I0752995

COOL CAT BLUES

Popular Music History
Series Editor: Alyn Shipton, Royal Academy of Music, London.

This series publishes books that extend the field of popular music studies, examine the lives and careers of key musicians, interrogate histories of genres, focus on previously neglected forms, or engage in the formative history of popular music styles.

Published

An Unholy Row: Jazz in Britain and its Audience, 1945–1960
Dave Gelly

Being Prez: The Life and Music of Lester Young
Dave Gelly

Bill Russell and the New Orleans Jazz Revival
Ray Smith and Mike Pointon

Chasin' the Bird: The Life and Legacy of Charlie Parker
Brian Priestley

Cool Heat: Anita O'Day and Her Dangerous Jazz Life
James Gavin

Dancehalls, Glitterballs and DJs: From the Pleasure Garden to the Discotheque
Bruce Lindsay

Desperado: An Autobiography
Tomasz Stańko with Rafał Księżyk, translated by Halina Maria Boniszewska

Eberhard Weber: A German Jazz Story
Eberhard Weber, translated by Heidi Kirk

Formation: Building a Personal Canon, Part 1
Brad Mehldau

Handful of Keys: Conversations with Thirty Jazz Pianists
Alyn Shipton

Hear My Train A Comin': The Songs of Jimi Hendrix
Kevin Le Gendre

Hidden Man: My Many Musical Lives
John Altman

Ivor Cutler: A Life Outside the Sitting Room
Bruce Lindsay

Jazz Me Blues: The Autobiography of Chris Barber
Chris Barber with Alyn Shipton

Jazz Visions: Lennie Tristano and His Legacy
Peter Ind

Kansas City Jazz: A Little Evil Will Do You Good
Con Chapman

Keith Jarrett: A Biography
Wolfgang Sandner, translated by Chris Jarrett

Komeda: A Private Life in Jazz
Magdalena Grzebalkowska, translated by Halina Maria Boniszewska

Lee Morgan: His Life, Music and Culture
Tom Perchard

Lionel Richie: Hello
Sharon Davis

Long Agos and Worlds Apart: The Definitive Small Faces Biography
Sean Egan

Mosaics: The Life and Works of Graham Collier
Duncan Heining

Mr P.C.: The Life and Music of Paul Chambers
Rob Palmer

Out of the Long Dark: The Life of Ian Carr
Alyn Shipton

Ray Brown: His Life and Music
Jay Sweet

Rufus Wainwright
Katherine Williams

Scouse Pop
Paul Skillen

Song for Someone: The Musical Life of Kenny Wheeler
Brian Shaw and Nick Smart

Soul Unsung: Reflections on the Band in Black Popular Music
Kevin Le Gendre

The Godfather of British Jazz: The Life and Music of Stan Tracey
Clark Tracey

The History of European Jazz: The Music, Musicians and Audience in Context
Edited by Francesco Martinelli

The Last Miles: The Music of Miles Davis, 1980–1991
George Cole

The Long Shadow of the Little Giant (second edition): The Life, Work and Legacy of Tubby Hayes
Simon Spillett

The Ultimate Guide to Great Reggae: The Complete Story of Reggae Told through its Greatest Songs, Famous and Forgotten
Michael Garnice

This is Bop: Jon Hendricks and the Art of Vocal Jazz
Peter Jones

This is Hip: The Life of Mark Murphy
Peter Jones

Trad Dads, Dirty Boppers and Free Fusioneers: A History of British Jazz, 1960–1975
Duncan Heining

Two Bold Singermen and the English Folk Revival: The Lives, Song Traditions and Legacies of Sam Larner and Harry Cox
Bruce Lindsay

Vinyl Ventures: My Fifty Years at Rounder Records
Bill Nowlin

Cool Cat Blues

The Life and Times of Georgie Fame

Ben Sidran

SHEFFIELD UK BRISTOL CT

Published by Equinox Publishing Ltd.

UK: Office 415, The Workstation, 15 Paternoster Row, Sheffield, South Yorkshire S1 2BX
USA: ISD, 70 Enterprise Drive, Bristol, CT 06010

www.equinoxpub.com

First published 2026

British Library Cataloguing-in-Publication Data
A catalogue record for this book is available from the British Library.
ISBN-13 978 1 80050 928 3 (hardback)
978 1 80050 929 0 (ePDF)
978 1 80050 930 6 (ePub)

Library of Congress Cataloging-in-Publication Data
Names: Sidran, Ben author
Title: Cool cat blues : the life and times of Georgie Fame / Ben Sidran.
Description: Sheffield, South Yorkshire ; Bristol, CT : Equinox Publishing Ltd, 2026. | Series: Popular music history | Includes index. | Summary: "Cool Cat Blues is the story of singer and pianist Georgie Fame. Born Clive Powell, in Leigh, Lancashire, he rose from being a troubled kid to the very top of the British pop charts. Through conversations and correspondence with Fame, as well as diligent research, Ben Sidran traces Fame's story"-- Provided by publisher.
Identifiers: LCCN 2026013482 (print) | LCCN 2026013483 (ebook) | ISBN 9781800509283 hardback | ISBN 9781800509290 pdf | ISBN 9781800509306 epub
Subjects: LCSH: Fame, Georgie | Singers--England | Keyboard players--England | Blue Flames (Musical group) | Musicians--England | LCGFT: Biographies
Classification: LCC ML420.F2345 S53 2026 (print) | LCC ML420.F2345 (ebook) | DDC 782.42164092 [B]--dc23/eng/20260326
LC record available at https://lccn.loc.gov/2026013482
LC ebook record available at https://lccn.loc.gov/2026013483

Typeset by Witchwood Production House Ltd

To the memory of Barry Ward
and the Bronte RSL Club in Sydney.

Contents

List of Illustrations

Preface

This book is based on conversations – in cars and planes and homes and hotels – wherever we happened to be together, for whatever reason – in Japan or Mexico, a recording studio in New York or a pub in Lancashire. From the beginning I believed that Georgie's story was the stuff of legend.

Georgie walks his own path and is not afraid to go where few have gone before, even if it means walking out on the wing of an aeroplane. Once when we were stuck in an enormous traffic jam between Berlin and Hamburg, without warning he jumped out of the car and began walking down the shoulder of the autobahn. I jumped out after him, leaving the driver to deal with the traffic, and together we walked along happily chatting about Louis Armstrong.

Ironically, we first met in Perth, Australia. It was at a jazz festival during the '80s; at that time, I knew his early records – "Yeh, Yeh", "Preach and Teach", "Pink Champagne" – but not the man himself. Meeting him and hearing him with the hard-charging Aussie Blue Flames was an epiphany: he was a musical force, a warrior, leaving it all on stage, taking no prisoners ... history made while you wait.

We became co-conspirators. I was starting a small record label and he signed up, becoming the first musician I produced for Go Jazz. Over the next few years we produced two more. It was a great achievement for us both when *Poet in New York* won the album of the year award from the French Académie du Jazz.

The same music – essentially Black American jazz and rhythm and blues – changed both our lives at an early age and in a permanent way. Music can do that: cross barriers, erase boundaries. Georgie had grown up in a small British mining town and I was raised in booming post-war America but it always felt to me like we were brothers in arms.

What emerges here is a picture of a man launched into the heart of a cultural revolution, holding close to music, his first passion and the object of his desire, for survival, legitimacy and honour. It is, at bottom, a tale about coming home, long after all the addresses have been changed.

Ben Sidran

1 Home

"Look, Clive, there's the dawn…"

Clive Powell was born on the 26th of June 1943 in a small terraced house, number 5 Cotton Street, in Leigh, South Lancashire. An industrial town nestled among neighbouring Wigan, Bolton and Warrington, Leigh is 12 miles west of Manchester and 22 miles east of Liverpool; it is in the geographic centre of the coal-mining and machine-weaving district of England, the heartland of the industrial revolution that arose in the 19th century.

His mother, Mary-Anne (also known as Dolly), was born at number 1 Cotton Street. His father, James, was born just a couple of miles up the road, in a small miner's cottage at the mouth of the Plank Lane coal pit. His father's father had moved there from the Welsh border at the turn of the 20th century to find work in the mines. Young Clive arrived into a close-knit family with deep roots in the local life; home and hearth meant everything to him.

His neighbourhood was known as "The Sportsman" because it was close to a pub of that name. At the back of the pub was a bowling green – not your average flat green but a beautifully manicured crown green that required technique if you wanted to master it – and just a couple of yards behind the green a wide canal that ran 80 miles between Leeds and Liverpool. In those days, immediately following World War II, the canal was busy with barges moving coal from the mines and depots all the way to Yorkshire: an impressive sight for any young lad.

Working in Leigh meant either going down into the coal mines or up into the cotton mills. Clive's mother was a cotton weaver and his father a cotton spinner, first in the Mather Lane factory and then at Bedford Mill, but the mines still dominated the imagination of children growing up on Cotton Street. That's because just one hundred yards from number 5 was the mouth of the Parsonage colliery; and, when sirens sounded, all the kids ran to the pithead to watch ambulances take away the injured miners on stretchers, their blackened faces covered in red blankets.

In the 1950s, both the factories and the mines ran 24 hours a day. The first shift ran from 6 am until two in the afternoon; the second, which they called the back shift, from two in the afternoon until ten in the evening; the last was the night shift, from 10 pm until 6 am. Clive's parents worked the first shift; while his older sister Evelyn went to school, he was left in the care of his grandparents who lived next door.

"Every member of the family who was capable had to work to see things through back then," he remembers. "During and after the war, there was rationing: each family was given a ration book by the government and whenever you wanted to buy something, you had to present the correct ration stamps. One was limited to how much butter or milk or vegetables and fruit you could have per week or per month."

He remembers his early childhood as being essentially carefree and happy. "We used to play in the streets, me and my friends – Winwood Hamer, Eddie Carney, Jackie Gornall, Vinnie Naughton and, a few hundred yards away, Frankie Parr and Wilf Clarke. There were several girls in our street gang too, the Mumford sisters and Jean Radcliffe." The gang spent most of their days playing in Cotton Street, playing cricket with a soft ball, fashioning a cricket bat from a broom handle and placing a dustbin against the kerb. Or they would play football on the streets until late into the evening after the lights had come on. There were gas lamps with glass mantles that came on at dusk, and more than once the gang was reprimanded for breaking a corner globe.

Just around the corner was a small shop run by the kindly Mrs Pasquil, who stocked whatever was available, tinned and fresh food, and a few hundred yards away were three fish-and-chip shops. Fish and chips was pretty much the staple diet in those days.

"We also had fantastic steak puddings," he says, "which were mincemeat in a suet casing with delicious brown gravy. You could have steak pudding and chips one day and you could have fish and chips another day. And there was a selection of pies. The favourite of most people was the meat and potato pie with chips. And with all these variations you could have sloppy peas – mushy peas as they now call them – which were real pigeon peas soaked overnight in bicarbonate of soda and then heated up so they lost their skins and became incredibly mushy."

Later on, he would be so nostalgic for this local food that he would leave the glamour of London and return home just to resample the tastes of his youth. He was a connoisseur of the local cuisine. "Nowadays you go into a restaurant and even fish-and-chip shops and they say they've got mushy peas on the menu but they're not *the* original mushy peas. They're processed [tinned] peas which they call mushy peas but they certainly don't taste the same."

Once he and the gang were old enough, they played at a disused coal pit about a mile away. "It was a huge slag heap which was almost in the shape of a volcano hill," he remembers. "We called it the 'Yoyo.' I don't know why we called it that because it looked nothing like a yoyo, but that's what we called it. We would walk or cycle to this hill and clamber up to the top. From there, we could see for miles.

"The hill was around 200 feet high, and from the top you could see well into Cheshire. You could see over the moors at the back of Bolton. You could even see to the back of Manchester. We would see stacks and stacks of little chimneys from the industrial sites. We probably counted 60 or 70 chimneys from the top of this hill, all of which were either from the coal mines or cotton factories. That was *it*, our horizon. There was nothing beyond that. There *was* nothing beyond that.

"Later, we used to cycle a couple of miles away until we were out into a little open space. All the towns were separated by a green belt, a small area where there were pathways and bramble patches. When I got my first bicycle," he remembers, "we'd go off blackberrying, particularly in September and early October.

"My father was a keen amateur ornithologist with a great knowledge of birds. By listening to the various birds he could actually identify them – just from their song and their whistles. I became really interested in bird life through my father. And flight. These were the kinds of fun things that were available to us in those days, before television."

Clive never knew much about his father's side of the family. His dad did have a half-brother, Fred, a coal miner who lived in Wigan. Fred was a heavy drinker, and every few months, when the family would be sitting in the kitchen, there'd be a banging on the front door. His mother would always recognize it as Uncle Fred's knocking. Fred had obviously been out to the Sportsman and, because he was in the neighbourhood, wanted to stop by before catching the last bus back to Wigan.

"My mother always said, 'Don't open the door, it's your Uncle Fred.' And we all had to sit there quietly until he would think there was no one home, or more likely that he wasn't going to be allowed in and he'd just disappear. Off he would trot."

Just around the corner on the road to Wigan was the Wigan Road Methodist Chapel, where the Powell family and almost all their neighbours went to church on Sunday, without fail, dressed in their Sunday best. This is where young Clive learned to sing the hymns: the start of his musical education.

He particularly remembers the "walking days": religious celebrations in which all the various churches in town – and there were many – would parade behind their own banner and maybe a brass band, culminating in a grand mass meeting in the marketplace in the centre of Leigh. People would make speeches and sing a couple more hymns, *en masse*, and then the crowds would disperse and everybody would walk back to their homes.

"One year," he recalls, "I couldn't have been more than five years old, and for some reason I got separated from my parents in the crowd. I don't remember being scared and there were only very few cars or automobiles in those days. But as the crowd thinned out I completely lost my family. And just then,

Photo 1: Georgie's mother and father, Mary-Anne and James.
Courtesy Clive Powell

a man and a woman in an open-top saloon car – quite a big car – noticed that I was stranded, lost, and they stopped and asked me my name. I told them, and I knew where I lived, number 5 Cotton Street, and they drove me home. I was rescued, much to my mother's joy. They'd already arrived home and were thinking about going back into town to the police station to report the fact that I was missing. I remember that adventure quite well."

At home his father liked to play the piano in a kind of stride style and he also played the accordion in a local dance band. Behind the church chapel, there was a hall with a small stage and an old upright piano at one end where they would hold dances. The band would consist of a drummer, a piano player, a saxophone player, with Clive's father on the accordion, and his Auntie Bessie the featured singer. Music was always the social lubricant in his life.

"My Uncle Jack, who was married to my Auntie Bessie, was a very fine tenor and Bessie was a great soprano and they sang wonderful duets together," he remembers. "They regularly sang in the church choir, and they also performed, as amateurs of course, for the Sunday School concerts. All my aunts would be there and all the people in the neighbourhood, including the children, would be there, having fun, playing games and learning to dance: slow foxtrots, valettas, quicksteps, palais glides, hokey-cokeys, you name it. Auntie Ada, who was the youngest sister in my mother's family, did a great deal helping me to learn how to dance at these Sunday School dance evenings, which were actually very, very enjoyable.

"I remember Rosemary Clooney's hit 'This Ole House', which was one of the first recordings I ever heard," he says. "And 'Mr Sandman' ('bring me a dream, make her complexion like peaches and cream'). That was one of the first tunes that I learned to dance to. There were also First World War tunes, waltzes mostly. 'Wedding Bells' was one of my favourites and it was written as if the soldier was singing: 'Don't worry, I'll be home from all this horror. And when I do come back, we'll get married.' In those days, the band would play medleys of three or four waltzes. It was just very romantic."

When Clive was seven years old, his Uncle Jack taught him to sing a song about a silver dollar – "You can roll a silver dollar down upon the ground and it will ro-o-oll because it's rou-a-rou-round" – and he also taught him all the actions that went along with it. By this time Clive had learned to play rickracks, or bones as they're called, and so he would sing, "...You can roll a silver dollar," with the rickracks in his right hand playing the rhythm and his left hand doing all the actions.

"This was a fantastic party piece for me," he says. "In fact, we used to go to various holiday camps in the area, particularly to the Isle of Man, which was a great summer treat. We would take a ferry from Fleetwood, just north of Blackpool, for our week's holiday. There was a holiday camp called Middleton Towers, in the north of Lancashire, where we went quite a few times.

"One summer my parents left me up in the chalet and went off to have their evening out with their friends and relatives. I don't know what came into me but I got out of the chalet and went to the main hall where there was an evening's entertainment going on. There was actually a talent contest which I entered wearing my short pants and plimsolls. I sang my party piece, 'You can roll a silver dollar,' with the rickracks and I got first prize. I won six shillings. And then my parents came in and saw me and I'm sure thought, 'What the hell is he doing here? He's supposed to be in bed.'"

His performance schedule increased dramatically after his Uncle Jack, who had been an RAF radio operator in the war, set up a microphone in the kitchen of 5 Cotton Street and ran wires into the front parlour, where all the friends and family would be gathered. He'd connect the microphone to the radio and anybody who was capable of doing something entertaining, whether it was reading a poem, singing a song or quoting some literature, would go into the kitchen and do their party piece, while everybody else was sitting in the parlour listening through the "wireless" that was perched on top of the fireplace. It was like a live broadcast, and it was the first of hundreds of radio appearances for him.

"My most abiding memory from those evenings of entertainment would be when our neighbour from across the street at number 4, Vinnie Naughton, came to sing. He was a few years older than me and had a wonderful singing voice and I'll never forget the sound of his voice coming through our wireless. He would sing a song made famous by Bing Crosby called 'Beautiful Dreamer', and I just thought it was the best singing voice I'd ever heard. And it was my neighbour from across the street!" All things seemed possible on Cotton Street.

There was rarely any alcohol involved. There might be a half a bottle of sherry or port in the corner cupboard but these could last half a year. Sometimes, after you'd done all your singing in church, you might retire home for tea and maybe have a little nip. But certainly not the youngsters. "I remember these evenings as being fantastic entertainment," he says, "and I suppose they were the bedrock of what was to come of me in the future."

His fondest memories are orchestrated by music. He remembers a day trip arranged by the Church Committee on a barge down the Leeds–Liverpool Canal. Everyone met up behind the Sportsman at the "Turning Bridge", an actual little wooden bridge that turned to allow the barges to pass through. They all piled onto the barge and floated from Leigh to Lymm in Cheshire, about 22 miles down the canal.

The trip took a full day and into the evening to get there and back; while they floated, his father took out his accordion and, sitting on the back of the barge, played old favourites like "Cruising Down the River (On a Sunday Afternoon)" while everybody sang along. "My dad was known, I think, in the fraternity as being a bit of a dreamer," he says. "He was inside himself quite a lot. He was a deep thinker, my dad was. But he could play – he could play."

His sister Evelyn took piano lessons, and took them very seriously, going all the way to the City of Manchester to take her final examinations. She could play complex, difficult pieces, but if you took the music away from her, "she couldn't play a note," Clive says. He too started with lessons around the age of six, from Mrs Whalley, one of his teachers at school, but he found the science of "the left hand reading the bass clef and the right hand reading the treble clef" frustrating. After a couple of months he gave up the lessons and started to teach himself to play by ear and by watching and listening to his father and sister. One of his sister's friends taught him how to play a simple boogie-woogie on the piano. He was so small he had to use two hands but he played it constantly. That simple musical pattern helped him win his first talent contest and launched his performing career.

So his musical education came from the combination of church sessions, family get-togethers and the occasional weekend away. The Methodist Church had properties in North Wales, where families could go and spend a weekend in a big mansion. "A bus would gather outside the chapel, everybody would sing a hymn, then get on the bus and drive through Warrington and Helsby into North Wales to a place called Plas-y-Nant. We'd spend the weekend walking in the countryside. Food would be provided," he says. "There would be Bible readings. And when it was time to go home everybody would congregate outside the building and sing one of these really warming hymns like 'Guide Me, O Thou Great Jehovah' and then back on the bus and home in time for Sunday evening." And, of course, come Monday morning everybody was back in the coal mine or the cotton factory.

"This was all an integral part of my growing up," he says. "I was a great respecter of authority. Never really got into any trouble. A few physical scrapes. I remember once at St Peter's School, which was the primary school, one of the guys in our class – his name was Jimmy Balmer and he lived just a couple of hundred yards up the road – he was a big lad, bigger than the rest of us. He wasn't particularly a bully but he did take advantage of his size occasionally. One day, he bullied someone in our class and, in my wisdom, I decided to stand up for the little man. We had a kind of fist fight, which entailed me going backwards all the way home. I remember going backwards fighting Jimmy Balmer with bare knuckles until we got home, where we called it even. I busted his lip and he busted my nose; didn't break it but there was blood on my nose. For 30 minutes I was slowly going backwards. I was punching him and he was punching me. I never made a forward movement in the whole fight. So there were the occasional scrapes like that, all good-hearted stuff.

"We were all firm rugby fans. The local sport in my hometown was rugby league, a great working-class game. It was strictly segregated in those days, not like it is nowadays. Rugby union was considered for toffs and educated people. If you belonged to a rugby union club or rugby league club, you couldn't visit or fraternize with members of the other code. You would be barred forever from your own code if you were caught fraternizing with members of the other code. Strikes me as crazy but that's how it was in those days.

"Since our code was rugby league it meant that rugby league players were considered professional. I mean it was a bit of a joke, because they only got like maybe £2 a week or something if they won, and less if they lost. So they all had day jobs and a lot of them, most of them, were coal miners. In fact, there used to be jokes around the rugby league fraternity: in places like Lancashire and particularly in smaller villages in Yorkshire they would say that people would holler down a mineshaft and say, 'Can you send us up a prop? We're short a prop forward for today's match.' It was a great game which actually knitted the community."

The Leigh team played at the Kirkhill Lane sports ground, which was a 20-minute walk from his home. On a Saturday, hordes of people, mainly men and boys, would stream through the neighbourhood to the rugby ground for home matches. The crowds could be enormous, 15,000–20,000, all bound together by tradition and local language.

"In our particular part of Lancashire, Leigh and Wigan, we had a very broad dialect," he says. "It was unintelligible outside the community. I mean if you went five miles down the road, they wouldn't be able to understand what you were talking about. It was really broad, with a lot of old English words in it like *thee, thine* and *thou*. A sort of typical North Country accent was like 'Up t'hill' ['up the hill']. Or, instead of saying, 'Where are you going now?' you'd say 'Wet doing now thee?' That was talking proper as far as we were concerned. So there was this totally different language going on up there."

Other weekends, he might take a shopping trip with his mother and one of her sisters to Manchester; the 12-mile journey would take about an hour on the bus. Or they would go to Bolton. "The great thing about going to Bolton," he says, "was the trolleybuses, which were electric, double-decker buses with a pole connected to a wire. They were way before oil became very popular. The wires were supported all the way from Leigh to Bolton and the trolleybuses were silent – literally silent. They were the same size as the double-decker buses but powered by electricity. You would take a number 82 trolleybus to get from Leigh to Bolton where they had a much bigger market than we had in Leigh."

But the Leigh market, which was only a 20-minute walk on a Saturday, was where he would find the greatest treat: something they called "duck and cake". It was really a rather rough pâté on a soft white roll (they called them "barm cakes"); "the pâté would be squashed into the soft barm cake/roll, and it was absolutely delicious. It was almost a square meal in itself. It was, I suppose, the equivalent of the hamburger today. But 'duck and cake' was fantastic."

In Leigh market there were stalls selling hundreds of items and at one such stall his mother bought him his first musical instrument: a harmonica. "Actually it was a mouth organ, and I was so overjoyed with this thing I played it non-stop until I could get a tune out of it. As I progressed on the mouth organ, a few weeks later at the same marketplace, she bought me my first chromatic harmonica, with a button on the side, which meant it had semitones on it. It was black and white, made of plastic and it probably cost about five shillings, if that. But this was my pride and joy and kept me happy for a year. I can remember walking the Wales countryside on one of our family weekend Sunday School outings and just going off with my harmonica playing in the wind."

The grandest national event to occur during his childhood was the Festival of Britain, an international trade fair to celebrate the best of British manufacturing and other industries, in the wake of World War II. It was held on a large site on the South Bank of the Thames in London, and central to the celebration was construction of the modernist Royal Festival Hall, which opened in May 1951 as a symbol of post-war optimism. Attending the opening was seen as a once-in-a-lifetime opportunity, and his whole family went to London for the weekend: a 12-hour coach trip from Leigh. That was his first experience on the London Underground. "I would have been eight years old and I remember – to my horror – my mother trying to get off one of the underground trains and the door closed on her. I was absolutely horrified thinking the doors were going to crush my mother. But of course they didn't; they just opened again.

"I don't remember where we slept for two days while we were in London," he says, "but I do remember on the coach journey back to Lancashire, which was an overnight trip, I slept on the floor in the aisle of the coach. And I remember we were maybe halfway on this journey, perhaps getting into Staffordshire, and the look of the sky: the first light was appearing and my sister Evelyn said to me, 'Look Clive, there's the dawn.' And I didn't know what dawn was – the word 'dawn' – what is dawn? This was my first experience of dawn, on this coach on the road to Lancashire from a weekend out at the Festival of Britain."

In September 1952, tragedy struck. He was not yet nine when his mother was taken into hospital. They said that she had an inflammation of her gall bladder, but it turned out to be cancer. In those days, children weren't allowed in the cancer ward, so he didn't actually see his mother in her dying months. Except once. One day his Uncle Jack took him to the hospital and insisted that the boy be allowed to see his mother. It was late November and Clive stood outside the ward while Uncle Jack argued his cause with the matron. Finally, he was allowed onto the ward and there, he says, "I remember standing by my mother's bed and she looked quite thin – she had always been a very buxom, boisterous lady, full of fun, with a wonderful laugh. And there she was lying in bed looking very drawn and thin.

"She didn't actually cry but there were tears welling up in her eyes. I was quite unaware of the seriousness of the situation. I didn't know what cancer was. And that was the last time I saw her. She died on December 2nd, 1952.

"The day she died. I was standing outside our house and my father came cycling down the road – because he would cycle to his factory job in those days instead of taking the bus. On his way back from his shift at the factory – he'd been allowed out a little early because of the seriousness of my mother's condition – he'd called in at the hospital. And she had passed away. I'm standing outside number 5 and I see my dad coming down the street on his bike. He briskly jumped off the bike, put it alongside the wall outside the house and looked at me – and I knew. He gave me a big hug. And that was it.

"Then we had to bury my mother. Her mother, Grandma Gillman, had died the year before. And in those days the casket was laid in the front room of the house and everyone paid their respects before the funeral service and the burial. I'd seen my grandmother lying in a casket and now it was time to see my own mother. We buried her in Leigh Cemetery."

His father had his factory job, of course, and his mother's parents, who had lived at 1 Cotton Street, had both recently passed away. And his sister Evelyn was 17 years old by then and had already started her first job at a factory just outside Manchester, taking the early bus every morning. So his Uncle Jack and Auntie Bessie moved into number 1 and did whatever they could to keep

Photo 2: Georgie aged six dressed as Charlie Chaplin.
Courtesy Clive Powell

the family on the rails. "I was more or less left to my own devices," he says. "It was rough."

"We never had carpet in our house in those days," he remembers. "We had linoleum on the floors. We never had a bathroom in our house. We had a tin bath that was hanging on the wall in the back yard which was brought into the kitchen and filled up with pots and kettles of hot water. That's where everybody took their baths. And for 18 months we didn't have a mother or a woman in the household to help.

"At the time, I had a dog I named Lucky, a sweet Golden Labrador. I have a photograph of me and him in a fancy-dress parade over in the Sunday School because my Uncle Jack used to dress me up in all kinds of gear. I remember him dressing me up as Charlie Chaplin once. I have a photograph of that. In one of these parades, I'm dressed up as a lion tamer and Lucky is the lion. Lucky loved my mum and, when she was taken to hospital, he started howling and fretting. He knew something was wrong. When my mother died, with all the pressure on the family and my father having to go to work, my sister having to go to a full-time job as well, and me barely going to school, my father decided to put Lucky down. It was terrible. I felt really attached to him and

I was devastated when he was destroyed. He was only like a year-and-a-half old. It was a terrible period."

For a brief while, his father sent him off to live with distant relations, the Hansons, a family that lived in Doncaster, over in Yorkshire. "I went and stayed over there for about a month at my dad's instigation," he says, "because it was the only thing he could think of. I was obviously acting a bit loopy. I was certainly vulnerable and unstable, and perhaps he thought it would be a good idea to get me off to another county to stay. But I didn't know these people, these relatives. They had two daughters older than me and a son pretty much the same age as me, nine or ten years old.

"I'll never forget when I was put on a bus to go there. Somebody came along with me, one of the family friends, I think, I don't know who, and took me to Manchester. And then they put me on another bus from Manchester to a town in Yorkshire called Barnsley where I had to change buses to get to Doncaster. Somebody was told to look after me to make sure I got the connection and I arrived in this town called Doncaster where I had never been. My relatives were waiting for me at the bus station.

"The next day, I remember we had breakfast of cereal, like corn flakes. And we had it with water because there was rationing in those days. You were only allowed a pint of mink or something per family for a day. They had a cat and the cat got the milk while the kids had their Kellogg's with water. I had never had it that way before but I had it that way every day. There I am, shipped out from home; my mother's gone and I'm stuck with these distant relations, having my cereal with water while the cat got the milk.

"When I got back to Leigh, I started to do all sorts of erratic things. Eventually, my Uncle Jack Gore – a coal miner who was married to my Auntie Ada and a great rugby player; he could run like the wind – he took me for a short walk around the park lake not far from where we lived and he was very considerate. I remember him talking to me and just trying to get my head straight over the fact that my mother had gone and that we all had to get on with life the best we could. And I'll never forget that pep talk, at the age of nine, walking round the lake with my Uncle Jack."

From time to time, he would also get "care packages" from his Uncle Joe, his mother's elder brother, the black sheep of the family. In 1947, Joe had decided to start a new life and took a boat from Liverpool to Canada. Clive remembers, though he was barely five, "The whole family went to Liverpool to see him off, and when he boarded the liner, we all drove under the River Mersey to New Brighton where we sat on a hillock as the boat departed – up the Mersey into the open sea. We all waved, saying goodbye to my Uncle Joe."

After a few years in Canada, Joe moved to California and found a job in the steel mills outside Los Angeles. It was from here he would send the care packages: big boxes full of American goods. While there was still rationing in England, these boxes, full of American biscuits and chocolates, made a huge impression on Clive. The best of all was when Joe sent him a baseball jacket.

"It was kind of pinkish colour and it fitted perfectly," he says. "I would walk around my hometown wearing this American baseball jacket feeling like a million dollars.

"I was wearing it the day I affected a broken arm at school. I basically just wanted to skip school. I was obviously still disturbed at my mother's death but didn't know it at the time, of course. I went to school with my baseball jacket and I put my right arm in a sling and wrapped my arm with cotton wool to make it look like plaster of Paris. We were all in the schoolyard before assembly, and my teacher came into the yard before assembly and said, 'What's up wi' thee?' Actually, he probably wouldn't have said 'thee' because they were more respectful in school, but perhaps 'What's wrong with your arm?'

"I said, 'I broke my arm, sir.' He put his fingers in and said, 'Well, it doesn't look broken to me.' And of course it wasn't. But I've never forgotten his kindness and his consideration because he didn't reprimand me at all over this. He must have been very understanding."

Not long after, Clive pretended to run away from home. His father and sister were out working at their day jobs, and he just skipped school. He filled a hessian sack with tins of baked beans, bread and one or two other things. Then he picked up a stray dog on the street and marched off toward the coal mine. He only got about a quarter of a mile when he arrived at the slag heaps at the back and decided he would camp out there. This was to be his new home, with a stray dog and a hessian sack full of provisions. He was discovered in a matter of hours and taken back home.

Life at home became complicated when, the following year, his father decided to marry a woman called Sally Bell. Sally was actually one of his mother's best friends from the Lilford Mill factory. She had a son, Derek, who was six months older than Clive, and she had lost her husband in a mining accident a year or two before. Since she and his father were in the same kind of predicament they decided to make a marriage of convenience.

"Derek and I had to sort of fit in, get along, yet we fought like hell. Not really serious fighting, just territorial stuff. I was never really comfortable with the fact that my father had married again. Even though later on I appreciated what Sally did for us. She was a very honest, hard-working woman and I think both of them needed partners."

Sally moved into 5 Cotton Street with Derek, and soon there were arguments as to how the house should be run. For example, his sister had started courting her future husband, Ken, a coal miner, and had announced that she'd like to get married. Sally hit the roof and read her the riot act, saying "You can't do anything until you're 21. You'll do as I tell you." There was a lot of animosity in the air and Clive couldn't wait to get out of the house.

When he was 12 he was allowed to do his first paper round, which meant getting up early in the morning, walking to the corner shop by the Sportsman pub, and shouldering a bag full of papers. "You would walk the paper round," he says. "If you could run it, you could probably get it done in 30 or

Photo 3: Rugby team, Leigh Central County Secondary School (also known as Windermere Road). Georgie is front and centre holding the ball. Team captain!

Courtesy Clive Powell

45 minutes. But it was a heavy bag full of newspapers that you delivered to all the houses in the local streets. Then you'd take your empty bag back to the Post Office and get off to school.

"Me and Frank Parr each had paper rounds and we'd walk off to school together, stopping off at a little miners' terraced shop outside the Parsonage Pit where Mrs Woodbine would allow us to buy a packet of two cigarettes, which we smoked on the way to school."

For Clive, school was memorable only because of the sports teams. "We had a cricket team and I played on the rugby team until the age of 15," he says. "Before I left school I ended up being the captain of that team, which was a great honour for me because I was in good company: Colin Tyrer played on that team and so did Frank Parr and both of those guys went on to become very, very good rugby league players representing not only local teams but Great Britain itself."

At the same time, while attending Windermere Road School, he got his first criminal record. Just outside the school there was a railway line that ran to Bolton and the boys had to walk over the railway bridge every day to get to school. The railway station was permanently closed, so several of the lads – there must have been 10 or 12 of them – decided to investigate. That is, they broke into the disused railway station and rifled the drawers. "It was just out of curiosity, really," he says. "It wasn't securely locked and we just rummaged around in there, finding old railway stamps for journeys and old papers and things relating to the railways and the railway station.

"We used to do this fairly regularly on our way home from school. We'd call in at the railway station, look around, rummage around, before carrying on home. One afternoon we left school, opened the door to the railway station and a big adult arm came out to grab one of us. It turned out to be the Railway Police. We all scampered and I remember running off down the railway line. I was pretty fast in those days but I was caught and so was my stepbrother, Derek. There were two others caught as well, brothers that came from a bit further up Wigan Road, in an area we called Cardboard City because the houses were kind of prefabricated.

"Eventually, out of the like 12 young boys that had all been nicked on this raid, my stepbrother and myself and these other two brothers were whittled down and taken to court, where we were accused of larceny, which is a pretty serious offence. We were like 12 or 13 years old. It was in the newspapers and it was quite a big scandal. We were severely reprimanded at home, of course. We were given conditional discharges. There was no fine or anything, just a conditional discharge, which means 'behave yourself and if you don't get into further trouble it's wiped from the record'. But that was a big scandal for us and I took it as a blot on my character, because, as I said, I was always a great respecter of authority."

That same year, trouble found his whole generation. It was 1956, the year when along came first Elvis and then Bill Haley's "Rock Around the Clock" and the film *Blackboard Jungle*. "I can remember going to school one day and two of my mates told me they had heard about the film, which was banned in our hometown," he remembers. "It was banned in a lot of places because, when it played in London, the Teddy Boys ripped up the seats and all that kind of thing. But it was being shown in Manchester and these two friends of mine told me they were going to play hooky and go to Manchester because they just had to see this film. A few days later, they didn't turn up for school and I knew where they had gone. When they came back the next day, they said, 'You won't believe it!' And that was it.

"I started to play truant. My dad and stepmother would go to work early. She'd leave at seven o'clock in the morning and I'd get up at seven for a bit of breakfast. I was supposed to leave for school at 8:30 for a nine o'clock start. But after I'd left the house, I'd climb back in through the window. I wouldn't go to school. I'd climb in through a little pantry window and hang around home playing piano.

"One day I was spotted by a neighbour and my stepmother was notified. About 9:30 in the morning, my stepmother came back from the factory and there I was, playing the piano in the front room. I was severely reprimanded. I think by then it was clear in her mind that music was going to be the ruin of me."

He had one good friend on the staff of the Windermere Road School. "Tommy Isherwood was my favourite teacher because he dealt with the sports. I remember when most of my contemporaries had left school and, because of my birthday in June, I had to stay on until the summer break; and so for the last three months I did very little academic work. Tommy would sort of ask me to look after the gym kit and all the rugby kit and the cricket kit. So I spent most of the time in this room like blowing up rugby balls, polishing and oiling cricket bats and making sure that all the kit was in good nick. He would even send me off to the school rugby ground, which was at the back of the pit, to inspect the pitch to see if it was playable for an upcoming match or something."

And, while he wasn't doing much academically, he was invited to organize the school Christmas Concert, where he played guitar and sang a song composed by Lionel Bart called "Butterfingers." Because he could play piano, he accompanied all the other kids in school who were doing "turns", singing or performing. Between sports and music, he gradually started to find his footing.

Sports was a hobby – although at one point he did think about trying to become a professional – but he was well on his way to becoming a professional musician. "There was a local theatre in our town, the Leigh Theatre," he says. "When I was a child, it was a legitimate theatre, and I went there to see a circus on the stage, with actual real live lions – or maybe just one lion in a cage. But the theatre itself ceased to function as a theatre in the mid '50s and was turned into a dance hall. They changed the name to the Casino – it became known as the Leigh Casino – and it became the premier gig and the place for teenagers to go for weekend dances.

"I started to play the piano there in all seriousness with the advent of rock 'n' roll. At the age of 14, I had heard Jerry Lee Lewis and Fats Domino on the radio. These were my main protagonists. And there was a wonderful recording by the great British jazz musician and musicologist Humphrey Lyttleton called 'Bad Penny Blues'. This recording featured a very heavily recorded boogie-woogie piano by a man named Johnny Parker, with which I was familiar thanks to my sister's boyfriend. I became obsessed with this record. I loved this record. Humphrey Lyttelton played sparse muted trumpet so the piano dominated the whole recording. And I think you'll find that Paul McCartney's composition 'Lady Madonna' was heavily influenced by Johnny Parker's boogie-woogie on 'Bad Penny Blues'."

When he finally left school in 1958, he was faced with either a job in a coal mine or a job in the cotton factory. Growing up, he had seen the occasional carnage at the pithead and decided, even though the money was better and quicker in the mine, to opt for the cotton factory.

At 15 he took a job in the Lilford Mill weaving factory, just over the canal from where he lived, working the first shift and learning how to look after the machinery. "Actual weaving was a woman's job. My mother, my stepmother and all the ladies in the area were all weavers. But men had to learn the rudiments of weaving, how everything worked, in order to become tacklers, which was a kind of engineer/maintenance man who took care of the actual looms in the factory and repaired them when necessary. You had to go to night school to learn about the engineering side of the industry. Then, when you were 18 years old, you were allowed to become an apprentice tackler and work on the night shift. You had to wait until you were 21 until you were fully qualified. It was a full apprenticeship.

"I used to go to night school in Leigh once a week to learn the engineering side of weaving. One day, I was probably not taking the lesson too seriously and the man in charge said to me, 'Powell, come to the front. You're never going to be a tackler if you don't concentrate on the work in hand. What do you want to do with your life?' And I said, 'Actually, sir, I want to be a musician,' and he laughed at me." That was his last visit to the night school.

Coupled with the advent of rock 'n' roll, "Bad Penny Blues" and all the songs he had learned from his father, he had developed a nice little repertoire and he began playing in a local pub, the Forrester's Arms. It was just him at an old piano, by himself, "No accompaniment whatsoever."

"The pub was a couple of miles out of town. You had to take a bus to get there," he remembers. "They'd be queuing up outside the pub on a weekend because they knew they were going to have a good night out. I wasn't allowed to drink any alcohol at all, of course – I was barely 15 years old – but on Friday night when I was playing in this pub, everybody would have a great time.

"One particular guy would get up every weekend and sing 'Among My Souvenirs', with alternative, ribald lyrics. I had to accompany him. I've never forgotten that tune. The rock 'n' roll thing was just coming in, and I could get away with Buddy Holly and Jerry Lee and Fats Domino songs. And because of my father and the stride piano he played, I could also play some of those old tunes like 'Who's Sorry Now?' with a kind of stride feeling, good enough to play in the pubs."

Now he was playing the whole issue, from rock 'n' roll to traditional music, and singing most of it as well. And everybody was singing along because he was playing tunes that they all knew – even oldies like "Ma, He's Making Eyes At Me" were known by the younger crowd, but he favoured the Johnny Otis arrangement, with a serious New Orleans feel to it.

In those days, he wasn't particularly distracted by girls. "Maybe," he speculates, "I was too young for girls. Or perhaps I never had the time. Or maybe it went back to my mother's passing. There were plenty of girls around, but I was only interested in playing and singing. I never got flash or big-headed about the whole thing, but when I took a bus out of town to the pubs that I played, on a Friday night or Saturday night, the bus would be absolutely jam-packed with me on board; and, when we got to the bus stop where the pub was, the bus emptied.

Photo 4: Georgie's first band, the Dominos, at the Leigh Casino, 1958. Left to right: Kenny Fillingham (guitar), Eric Eastham (drums), Johnny Hodgkinson (lead vocal), Clive Powell (piano), Ronnie Carr (guitar, leader).
Courtesy Clive Powell

"I was getting a bit of a reputation, locally, and enjoying myself, out of school and being a bit daring at weekends. I had started playing with three other like-minded young men from the neighbourhood. We had a little skiffle band called the Satellites, with the tea chest bass, with the string and the broom handle, two guitars, and one guy with a snare drum, and of course me at the piano. That didn't last very long because I was approached by Ronnie Carr who invited me to join the Dominos, the number one band in town. Their residency was at the Leigh Casino where all the kids went.

"My stepmother was never too happy with this other occupation that I had found, even though I was still doing okay and behaving myself. In her eyes, I was gallivanting away at weekends: there was a dance hall in Atherton called Formby Hall, a couple of miles out of town, where I started to play. It was then that my stepmother started to impose a curfew, saying that if I was going out playing with these bands in these pubs at the weekends – I mean she was a real strict Victorian type – then I had to be home at a certain time. I think she imposed a 10 pm curfew.

"One evening, it was winter – it must have been January – and the Dominos had a gig at the Formby Hall, Atherton. By the time I got home it was probably about 11 o'clock and the doors were locked. I couldn't get into the house. All the windows were locked because once or twice before, when I was a bit late, I'd climb through the pantry window, creep upstairs to my bedroom and nothing was said.

"But this night even the pantry window was locked and I had to spend the whole cold January night sitting in our outside toilet – we didn't have an indoor bathroom in those days. I spent the whole night out there in a freezing toilet and I started to get a bit angry. My dad finally came out early in the morning and said, 'Come on son. In you go.'"

Clearly, the fact that Clive was beginning to play locally was becoming a source of great antagonism to his stepmother Sally, and she became increasingly disturbed by the fact that he was taking music seriously. Things in general were getting uncomfortable at home. She was doing her best to make sure he didn't go off the rails, but in his own mind he was already out of town. "I can look back at those things now with humour," he says. "But when I was sitting in that freezing toilet all night, I was thinking, 'Right, I'm going to do something about this.' It made me more determined, whenever the chance came, to take it."

In the meantime, he took his satisfaction on stage with the Dominos. He was young – two years younger than everybody else in the band – and there was a great lead singer in the band: a local guy called Johnny Hodgkinson, who had a fantastic voice, a bit like Little Richard. The group was definitely happening.

They had quite a lot of work in the local working men's clubs and occasionally played at Burtonwood, the American Air Force base near Warrington. "Which was actually like visiting another planet," he says, "because they had their own entertainment set-up. You could walk in and they had Coca-Cola and all these things we'd never seen: fantastic steaks and food and luxuries, as far as we were concerned."

He had been drawn to the Burtonwood Air Force base years earlier. He had ridden his bike there as a child, about a nine-mile ride, to go plane spotting. It was just after the Korean War and the frontline American aircraft in those days was the F56, called the Super Sabre. Clive would sit on a hillock overlooking the runway watching these F56s taking off and landing – thinking of flying himself one day.

On his trips to Burtonwood, he had to pass through Warrington, and just outside of Warrington was the Royal Air Force boot camp called Padgate. Many years later he realized that, as he was cycling past Padgate in 1957 on his way to do some plane spotting, Bill Wyman, the Rolling Stones' bass player, would have been inside doing his Royal Air Force National Service. So many of the roots of British rock 'n' roll were in this part of England, in the heart of the North.

In the summer of 1959, when he was 16, he and a couple of older friends booked themselves on a summer holiday to the Butlin's holiday camp in North Wales; it was his first trip away without his parents. They had booked chalets and were going to stay for a week.

By this time, he was a fairly accomplished musician and had been playing regularly in local pubs; so, when they got to the camp, he was encouraged by his mates to perform in the local pub. He would get up and sing something by Jerry Lee Lewis or Fats Domino and, in his words, "Everybody would go, 'Yeah!'"

Then, one night, there was a talent contest at the camp. He entered and strolled his way through the heats – "It was dead easy," he says, "there was really no competition." The day before the final round, he was approached by Rory "Shakes" Blackwell, a professional rock 'n' roll bandleader from London who was working at the camp for the summer season. The moniker was bestowed on him because he would actually shake all over while singing certain songs, which at the time was a very effective gimmick. He told Clive his lead guitar player had just been caught in a chalet with a member of the opposite sex – there were very strict rules about fraternizing if you were employed by Butlin's – and outright asked him if he would like to join the band. Clive was definitely interested but there was a catch.

"I said to Rory, 'You know, I've got a job in a factory back in Leigh and you'll have to talk to me mam and dad about this because they might not be too happy.'" He withdrew from the final stage of the talent contest because it was strictly for amateurs and he had just been invited to become a professional; when he withdrew, a young man named Richard Starkey – or Ringo Starr as he would later be known – was the winner, along with a singer from Liverpool. To this day, Clive believes he could have won the contest in a walk had he stayed in.

Rory was so keen to employ him that he drove Clive all the way back to Leigh. "My father and my stepmother had already returned from their holiday," he remembers, "and she was there doing the ironing. She'd already heard the news that I'd been offered a job. God knows how the news passed so quickly. This would probably be on a Sunday after the holiday had ended and Rory Blackwell had driven me from Wales and my stepmother knew all about it."

Rory spent the whole day in the house with Clive's parents trying to convince them that he would look after the boy. At the time, Clive was earning £2 15s. (two and three-quarter pounds in pre-decimal money) a week as an apprentice weaver and Rory Blackwell was offering him £12 a week as a professional musician at the camp, where all food and accommodation was free. It was a pretty fantastic step-up in earnings. His father was quite sympathetic but his stepmother would have none of it. Finally, after spending the day trying to convince them, Rory said, "Well look if you decide you want to do it, the job is there. All you have to do is send me a telegram or call me and you can have the job."

His stepmother was so upset that Clive spent the following week sharing a bed with his father. "She was adamantly against this idea," he says. "I was confused. I went back to my job at the factory on Monday, and the whole factory knew about this predicament. All the women in the factory knew my mother and my stepmother – they'd all been workmates together all their working lives – and half of the women in the factory were saying to me, 'What do you want to go gallivanting off down London for, or to Butlin's, playing the piano? This is your life in this factory. This factory will never close. This is your home. This is where all your family are. Why do you want to go and do something stupid like that?' And the other half of them were saying to me, 'You'll never get another chance like this, lad. Take it.'"

He took a week to weigh the pros and cons and then one evening, being a great respecter of authority, he walked into the police station in town and told the desk sergeant the whole story. He said, 'Look I've just turned 16 years old. I've got a job at Lilford factory. I've been offered this job as a professional musician at Butlin's in North Wales, and my stepmother is threatening me with the police. She said she'd have the police on me if I decide to take up this job and go away." The sergeant said, "Well you're 16. If you do it and you behave yourself, don't get into any kind of trouble with the law, there's nothing we can do about it." That made him decide.

He went back home and confronted his stepmother. He told her, "I've been to the police and you can't do anything to me. So I'm going to do it." But, in the end, he did say, "Just give me two months. If it doesn't work out, I'll come back to this job in the factory and I'll be what I've always been and continue to live up here, or whatever my destiny was."

So he telegrammed Rory Blackwell at the holiday camp and said, "I'm coming." He packed a little suitcase and his brother-in-law, Ken, drove him out of town.

2 The Road

"Forget the shoe! They're gonna kill us!"

At Butlin's, he was paid £12 a week but only spending £4. The rest went into his Post Office savings account. He felt like he was on the way to becoming quite well off. It was at Butlin's that he met his first serious girlfriend, a "redcoat", employed by the camp, named Renie McCargo, from Glasgow. She was good-looking, with "a very nice character", and she took his virginity. "I was very happy about that," he remembers.

About three weeks after Clive had arrived, Rory Blackwell was invited to a party at a disused Air Force base a few miles from the camp. On the way back he crashed his car and was injured. It wasn't a hospital case but he couldn't perform his duties as the frontman of the band. He was walking with a stick so he couldn't dance, and he certainly couldn't do the shake; he even had trouble singing. The entertainments manager of the camp, a Mr Bamford, came into the dance hall one night to find Rory under-performing whereupon he was instantly fired, along with Clive and the rest of the band.

"I'd only been there three weeks and the ceiling fell in," Clive remembers. "I'd promised my parents – after all the arguments and deliberations – that I'd give this job a go and if it didn't work out after a couple of months, I'd come back to Leigh with my tail between my legs and get my job back in the factory – at least I'd tried.

"There I was, facing impending disaster and Rory says, 'Well, let's all go down to London', because the other members of the band were all Londoners. He said, 'I've got plenty of work down there.' And I thought, 'Okay, great, I've only been to London once, for the Festival – so let's go.' So we took the train down from North Wales to London. That was another long ride and the train was full. We were sitting on suitcases for about 15 hours. The train arrived at Paddington Station and I was billeted with the drummer who lived with his parents in Kentish Town. Rory said, 'Sit tight. I'll get all the work sorted out and I'll come and see you.'"

But the work never materialized. Rory found a couple of derelict rooms for Clive above a small ballroom in Islington, just off Upper Street, near Canonbury Square, which became his first accommodation in London. Next door was a Turkish Cypriot café where he could order egg and chips. "It had a jukebox," he says, "which always seemed to be playing Paul Anka's recording of 'Diana', which I loved. Apart from the one in the US Air Force base, that was the first jukebox I'd ever heard."

For a time, he was quite happy eating his egg and chips and listening to Paul Anka. There was also a fish-and-chip shop around the corner, but it didn't really agree with him. In Lancashire they used cod or haddock but in London it was rock salmon. He'd tried it and didn't like it, so he didn't get on with the London chippies. But he had plenty of time on his hands to keep the search going.

Time passed and work still didn't materialize. Rory appreciated the predicament Clive was in and eventually found him a job playing solo piano in a pub in the East End, in Canning Town, right on the docks. In order to get to the gig Clive had to take three buses (actually, one bus and two electric trolleys like they had in Lancashire). He'd be playing the old pub songs, mixing in the rock 'n' roll tunes and then passing the box around; there were no formal wages playing for the dockers. At the end of the night, he would take the three buses back to his little place in Islington.

After a month or so, Rory announced that Larry Parnes had arranged a summer season up in Blackpool for the band. Parnes was the first major rock manager in Britain and his stable of artists included most of the successful singers of the day. His first big artist was a young man whose name was Tommy Hicks until Parnes changed it to Tommy Steele. Steele became a huge star, and Parnes bestowed new names on all his other young singers. He came up with the names Johnny Gentle and Billy Fury, and he changed Reg Smith's to Marty Wilde.

Marty had just fired both his bass player, Tex Makins, and his drummer, Bobby Woodman, for some indiscretion they had committed, forcing them to abandon their summer season in Blackpool. "They came down to London and somehow contacted Rory," says Clive, "and Rory thought these guys were rock 'n' roll stars. They probably were because they had played with a big rock 'n' roll star, Tommy Steele. They had bleached blonde hair and Rory announced, with great excitement, 'These guys are coming down from Blackpool. They're gonna join the new band and we're going to get all the work that's going.' Fantastic!

"I'm sitting up in my dilapidated room, above the dance hall, the Strava Ballroom as it was called, and down from Blackpool comes Tex Makins and Bobby Woodman. They walk in, take one look at me and say, 'We'll have to do something about that, for a start.' They sat me down in a chair in front of a mirror and proceeded to peroxide my hair blonde, because in order to be in that band I was going to have to have bleached blonde hair. I'm sitting there thinking what the hell are these guys doing to me? But they bleached my hair. So there were three of us: bass, drums and piano. We must have had a guitar player too – I can't remember who – and Rory was singing.

"The first gig we played was downstairs in the Strava Ballroom. Nobody came. It turns out the only people that ever came to the Strava Ballroom, as far as I saw, were there because it was also used as a rehearsal room for a very popular British rock 'n' roll TV show, the *Oh Boy!* show. It was a fantastic rock 'n' roll show in those days, but for some reason I was never around when they were so I never got to see any of these great early rock 'n' roll singers rehearsing. I was going to be working with them in the very near future, but at the time there was nothing happening. There was no work.

"We played in a couple of other dance halls around Islington, which were fairly violent. I mean, the band never got involved, but it was pretty uncomfortable for a 16-year-old lad from Lancashire. So Rory got me a gig in the Essex Arms in Silvertown Way, where I was happy to play. The landlord, who drove a silver Bentley, took pity on me. He realized that I was just this 16-year-old, bleached-blonde kid playing in his pub and then taking buses all the way back through East India Dock Road, through the East End of London, late at night to get back to his bed in Islington. So he allowed me to sleep in the pub. I can't remember how long I played there. It might have been as long as a month or so.

"Rory, to his eternal credit, was always concerned about my welfare and he arranged an audition for me with Larry Parnes, who had a monopoly on the scene and was organizing these fantastic rock 'n' roll package tours. This was September 1959. I'd only left the Butlin's camp six weeks before but it seemed more like a lifetime.

"I remember going from my room in Islington, taking three buses down to Lewisham in South London to the Lewisham Gaumont. I stepped off the bus outside the theatre and there was this huge notice outside saying 'The Marty Wilde Show!' with all these other rock 'n' roll names – lesser known than Marty, but all involved in this rock 'n' roll package show. I walked round the back, knocked on the stage door and said, 'I've got an audition for Larry Parnes.' Somebody took me in the wings. The show was in progress. Larry Parnes was standing there. He looked at me and he went, 'Er, yes, who are you?' I said 'I'm Clive Powell.' I had a very thick Lancashire accent, 'and Rory Blackwell arranged this audition for me.' He said, 'Er, mm, yes, we'll call you Clive Wells and you can go on after this next number.'

"So I thought, okay. There's a band on stage backing another singer – it turned out to be Colin Green and the Beat Boys – and totally unannounced, I walked out to the piano, said to the rest of the band, '"High School Confidential" in F' and commenced to sing the Jerry Lee Lewis tune. I knew it note for note, and they knew it because everybody knew Jerry Lee Lewis tunes. All the rock 'n' roll tunes of the day, the bands were hip to them. I walked off and that was it – I got the job."

Photo 5: The Larry Parnes era: 1959.
Courtesy James Powell

Larry Parnes said to him, "Okay, you start the next tour in Birmingham," which was to leave in October, and this was already late September. Clive dashed up to Lancashire and told his folks that he'd actually secured a job as a piano player with Larry Parnes, the greatest impresario in Britain, and he was going to be touring the country playing all these big theatres, backing people like Duffy Power, Tony Sheridan and all these exotically named singers. And by the time he had finished telling his parents the good news, their whole attitude had changed. "Suddenly," he says, "I was going to become something that they could be proud of. I was even going to get my name in the papers very, very soon. Not only the local papers; I was going to be in all the papers very, very soon."

And so in October 1959 he started his first tour with the Larry Parnes Organisation as a piano player named Clive Wells, backing all the greatest rock 'n' roll stars of the day. The routine was always the same: the tour coach would show up at Marble Arch outside Larry Parnes's apartment and everybody would rendezvous there and off they would go. Apart from the one-nighters, they did full weeks in big theatres like the Liverpool Empire, the Ardwick Hippodrome in Manchester, the Birmingham Hippodrome and the Glasgow Empire.

"This was really big-time stuff for a young kid," he says. "I can remember when we first played at the Liverpool Empire, the Beatles and all the great Liverpool bands that made names for themselves in the early '60s were in the audience. I was playing with Tony Sheridan and, after that first night, the Liverpool football fans took up Tony Sheridan's version of 'You'll Never Walk Alone' and it became a famous football anthem.

"After the show, there was a knock on the stage door and the stage doorman came and found me and said, 'There's a bloke outside who wants to see you named Richard Starkey,' who was Ringo, of course. He was just keeping in touch after the brief meeting that we had at the Butlin's holiday camp a few weeks earlier. I got him in backstage and we sat on the backstairs talking about the music and the possibilities and how here I am, suddenly, you know, a few weeks out of Butlin's and I'd landed this fantastic job with all these great British rock 'n' roll stars. My family and friends, everybody, was immensely proud of me. They'd all turn up at these gigs whenever we played within 30 or even 50 miles of Leigh."

He was on his way but still living day-to-day. He was making £20 a week but had to pay all his own expenses out of that. "When we arrived at a town like Liverpool," he says, "the first thing we had to do was to go out and find accommodations, which would be in 'bed and breakfast' houses, not hotels. We couldn't afford hotels, but there were lots of B&Bs around; and older members of the band would have places they would recommend. We'd set ourselves up in some friendly B&B and that would be our home for the week while we played to thousands of screaming fans in all these great big theatres around England."

At the time, Larry Parnes was having altercations with one of his artists, Chris Morris from Liverpool. Parnes had given him the next exotic name on the conveyor belt: "Lance Fortune". But "Lance" had left the Larry Parnes Organisation after a few weeks to set up his own career with his own management – he didn't want to be part of the Parnes system anymore – and taken the name with him. Larry was really peeved about this. "How dare somebody walk off with *my* name, the name that I've given this next artist?" In an attempt to reclaim ownership of the name, Larry decided that Clive would become "Lance Fortune" on the tour in the hope that the other Lance Fortune would relinquish it.

The *Daily Herald*, one of the big national papers in England at the time, wrote, "Will the real Lance Fortune please stand up?" against photographs of both Clive and Chris Morris. This little vendetta only lasted until Chris Morris's song "Be Mine" entered the British Hit Parade – not to the top but enough to make the top 20 and force Larry Parnes to concede.

Soon after – in late 1959 or early 1960 – Larry Parnes came sidling up to Clive on the band bus and said, "I've got a new name for you. You remind me of George Formby (a legendary music hall and film star, with a thick Lancashire accent like Clive's). My new name for you is Georgie Fame."

And Clive said to Larry, "What's wrong with my real name?" And Larry said, "If you don't use my name, I won't use you in my show."

"Obviously it was a very important gig to have, to be on stage with all these British rock 'n' roll stars," says Clive, "fantastically glamorous and well paid, and I'm still only 16 years old. So I swallowed my pride. I thought, "It's a name, what the hell!" And from then on I was Georgie Fame."

The tours usually only lasted two or three weeks and then there'd be a two- or three-week break. Georgie had rented himself a room for a couple of quid a week in a house in Islington – Islington was still the only area of London that he was familiar with – number 208 in Liverpool Road. It was a nice house owned by a friendly and welcoming Greek Cypriot family, the Christies. He was happy to finally have his own independent situation, a room with a small electric cooker; and that became his home base in London when he wasn't on tour.

But often, when he got a break from the tour, he'd go back to Lancashire and spend time with family and friends, playing bowls on the green at the back of the Sportsman, having a couple of pints at lunchtime, living on his favourite childhood fare from the fish-and-chip shops. When it was time to go back on tour, he'd take the train down to London and get the bus from Marble Arch.

In early 1960, Larry Parnes made a decision that would have a profound impact on Georgie's life. He decided to bring over two American rock 'n' roll stars, Gene Vincent and Eddie Cochran, and put out a tour that Georgie was going to be part of. Now he was part of the Larry Parnes stable with his new name, he was allowed to sing one song every night at the start of the show; the rest of the time he was backing the other singers. The early posters for this tour displayed his new name down on the bottom right-hand side: "Georgie Fame, new singing pianist".

Before the tour started, they were all called to a rehearsal in Soho so that Gene Vincent and Eddie Cochran could decide who was going to play with whom and what songs were going to be performed. When the musicians walked into this basement room, there was Eddie Cochran sitting on a stool, cross-legged, Gretsch guitar in hand, leather waistcoat and cowboy boots.

Photo 6: Georgie in 1960 with Gene Vincent.
Courtesy James Powell

Marty Wilde's band, the Wildcats, and Georgie and Colin Green and the other Beat Boys gathered around. Eddie Cochran asked, "Anybody here ever heard of Ray Charles?" Nobody put their hand up.

Cochran commenced to play the rhythm to "What'd I Say" on the guitar and sang a couple of choruses. Nobody had ever heard anything like it in the UK before that moment. When Eddie Cochran, a charismatic artist and a great guitar player, played the song that day, they all went bananas. "It wasn't till a few weeks later," Georgie remembers, "that we heard the original version by Ray Charles, with the introduction that Eddie had played (which Ray Charles originally played on the Wurlitzer piano). When we first heard that record nobody knew what the instrument on the intro was, because we hadn't heard a Wurlitzer piano before. We thought it was some kind of special effect on a guitar, because Eddie had played it perfectly."

It was decided that the Wildcats, would be Eddie's backing group while the rest of the musicians would back Gene Vincent and the various other artists on the bill.

There was another band on the Eddie Cochran/Gene Vincent tour called Nero and the Gladiators, led by Mike O'Neill. Mike came from a little village outside of Leigh called Lowton, and had played solo piano in some of the pubs around Leigh just as Georgie had. He was five years older than Georgie and many more years hipper, and Georgie remembered seeing him walking around Leigh town centre wearing a dickie bow and calling everybody "Dad". He was a real jazz fan and a bohemian-type character.

Mike had formed Nero and the Gladiators with bass player Rod Slade, who became known as Boots – Boots Slade – because he was given a pair of boots by Eddie Cochran, which he wore with pride everywhere he went. Mike used to dress up as Nero, in a toga, with the rest of the band as Roman centurions, and they would sing and play rock 'n' roll. It was quite a successful act.

So off they all went, with Eddie Cochran and Gene Vincent, playing a week in Southampton, a week in Glasgow – a week here and a week there. They also did a series of one-nighters culminating in early April, just before the Easter weekend in 1960, with a week at the Bristol Hippodrome.

"When we did that first Eddie Cochran/Gene Vincent tour," says Georgie, everywhere we went future successful British artists would be in the audience. When we played in Cardiff, Tom Jones was in the audience. When we played in Liverpool, the Beatles were in the audience. Within three months of that first tour, every upcoming British band in the country was trying to play 'What'd I Say' like Eddie had played it. They were all playing it wrong and differently but at least they were on the way to getting Ray Charles."

Being on the road with Eddie Cochran and Gene Vincent was a wild ride for Georgie. Perhaps the most dramatic moment was the one-night stand they played at the Caird Hall in Dundee, Scotland. Caird Hall was an old concert venue with a traditional music platform – no curtains or anything, just a low stage – and that night the place was packed with 1,500 people. Eddie Cochran always closed the first half of the show and Gene Vincent closed the second half.

Cochran always brought the house down: he'd already made a record covering Ray Charles's "Hallelujah I Love Her So", did a fantastic version of both "Milk Cow Blues" and "Fever" and, of course, he covered "What'd I Say". Normally there was an intermission and time for everybody to cool down between halves. But not in Dundee. At Caird Hall, when Gene Vincent took the stage for the second set, following only a brief pause, before he had sung more than a couple of tunes hordes of Scottish fans started slowly marching from the back of the hall towards the bandstand. When they reached the stage they simply invaded it.

Big Jim Sullivan, the guitar player, ran on stage and started tossing them back into the audience, two at a time; drummer Red Reece disappeared behind his kit, so shaken by the experience he was having a sip from his hip flask. Georgie was standing on stage at the piano when a young Scottish fan came running up to him. He felt certain a punch was coming, but all the fan wanted to do was shake hands and say, "Hey man that was fucking great." Gene Vincent disappeared under a pile of fanatical fans and was last heard saying, "Give me an E, give me an E!" He wanted to continue the show but there was no way they could.

The police closed it down and the next day the Scottish newspapers were full of news about this riot that had taken place at the Caird Hall. As far as the Scots were concerned, the biggest part of the disaster was that Caird Hall was named after the famous Scotsman Sir William Caird, whose bust had accidentally been smashed by the mob. It was quite a while before rock 'n' roll was ever permitted there again.

After the last gig of the tour, all the people involved – musicians, management and crew – made their way back to London. Eddie Cochran and Gene Vincent booked a private taxi to take them from Bristol to a hotel at London's Heathrow Airport, where, the next day, they were to fly back to the US. They would take a break before returning to England to continue on a second tour.

The taxi driving Eddie Cochran and Gene Vincent took the A420 road. On the outskirts of Chippenham, the driver lost control of the vehicle doing 60 mph and went off the road. Eddie Cochran was killed instantly.

Georgie, driving back to London in the van with the tenor saxophone player Billy McVay, had gone to London via Bath on the A4 and arrived very early on Sunday morning, unaware of what had happened up on the 420. The next day, Billy McVay had organized a gig for the Beat Boys and Georgie at a club in Southend in Essex. It was Easter Monday. When the band met up again at the Newbury Park tube station, they picked up a newspaper and there it was. The headline read: "Eddie Cochran killed in car crash!"

A few weeks later, Gene Vincent, who wasn't seriously injured in the accident, came back to England and Larry Parnes brought in another American singer, a relative unknown named Jerry Keller, as a replacement for Eddie. The tour continued down the road as if nothing had happened.

With Gene Vincent back, the band went into EMI studios at Abbey Road to record a single in conjunction with the new tour. Gene sang a song called "Pistol Packin' Mama", and the B-side was a country ballad called "Weeping Willow". It was Georgie's first recording session, and because he'd always played standing up – even in the local bands in Leigh – he did the whole recording session like that, as if it were a gig. The players on the date were Red Reece on drums, Colin Green on guitar and Vince Collard on bass. That recording made the British top 20; so, at the age of 16, Georgie Fame was in the charts.

Early in the tour, they played a week at the Birmingham Hippodrome. One of Larry Parnes's artists was a singer by the name of Dickie Pride, a raucous character and a consummate performer. He also did the shakes on stage like Rory Blackwell. "In those day," says Georgie, "we all wore a little bit of Max Factor make-up because of the stage lights and all that. It was part of the process: we thought we had to wear make-up. It was the 'done thing' in those days, just a little thing around the face." Bear in mind the British rock 'n' roll scene came out of a well-established music hall tradition.

On tour, each artist would sing three or four songs. In Birmingham, after his turn, Dickie went out of the stage door to the local pub for a quick drink, still with his stage make-up on. Two or three local guys in the pub made disparaging remarks about Dickie – they called him a "poofter" or something similar – who hit one of them in the face and then dashed back into the theatre.

"We didn't know anything about this until the end of the concert," says Georgie, "but when we finished the last number and tried to leave the theatre, we found we couldn't. There were like two hundred Birmingham Teddy Boys standing outside the stage door all baying for our blood. Our B&B was in a pub at Five Ways, about three-quarters of a mile down the road from the theatre. There was no way we could get out the backstage door – I think the police had been called. People were waiting around but Billy McVay and Clem Cattini, the drummer, and me decided that we could actually sneak out of the front of the theatre, and they wouldn't see us and we could make our way back to our B&B.

"So we snuck out the front of the theatre. It was working until we had to pass the street that led to the stage door. Unfortunately, these guys saw us and gave chase, so we legged it. We started running, and I was wearing a pair of casual Italian slip-on shoes. We're roaring along and suddenly I lost one of my shoes. I went back to get it and Clem screamed at me, 'Forget the shoe, forget the shoe. They're going to kill us! Keep going.' I ran back, got the shoe and took off. We could see the pub in the distance. We got to the door; it was just after closing time and they'd locked the door!

"We're banging on the door to try to get into the pub as this crowd of hooligans was getting closer and closer and closer. They probably got to within 30 yards of us and, thank God, the landlord opened the door. In we went, closed the door and that was the end of that."

Things like that happened more than once on tour: Teddy Boys would get jealous of their girlfriends becoming too excited about the music or the musicians and would wait around after the show to express their displeasure. But the popularity of the tours and the players continued to grow, riding a wave of rock 'n' roll fever that seemed to push aside everything in its path.

When Billy Fury became a big enough artist to demand his own band he selected four players from the pool of Larry Parnes musicians, including

Georgie, and called them the Blue Flames. It would be a name that Georgie would use for the rest of his career.

"I was the piano player," says Georgie, "Colin Green on guitar, Red Reece on drums and I think the first bass player might have been Vince Collard, as he called himself. We became Billy Fury and the Blue Flames, his exclusive backing group. No more playing for Duffy Power, Tony Sheridan or all the other acts; we were now playing solely for Billy Fury. We'd thought we'd really hit the big time.

"Billy was a great guy to work for, a sweet guy, great choice of material. He loved Ray Charles, of course. He loved Etta James and people like that and he recorded a couple of big hits. I was actually in the Decca recording studios in London when he recorded his hit 'Halfway to Paradise'. We weren't capable of playing on those records in those days. We were just his backing band, but I was in the studio the day he recorded it.

"We toured with Billy up and down the country. He had a road manager named Hal Carter, who was also from Liverpool, and the two of them drove the country in this fantastic little MG sports car that Billy had. We were relegated to a van, where we threw the drum kit and the bass and the guitar amps and our personal belongings and that's how we got around the country. This went on for quite a while.

"One summer we did a season of concerts every Sunday at the Great Yarmouth pier – which is on the Norfolk coast, on the east side of England. On the Saturday evenings prior, we would often have to do concerts miles away, like one in Chippenham in Somerset, Workington up in Cumbria or Prestatyn in North Wales. We'd play in these far-out places on a Saturday and then we'd be driven by this fantastic old chauffeur we called Cronin – Jim Cronin, I think his name was. He was a veteran of the Arnhem campaign, a distinguished soldier and a very nice man. But he was driving four 16- and 17-year-olds in the back and all they wanted to do on these night trips was drink Australian white wine and make a lot of noise. Poor fellow.

"Invariably, we'd arrive at Great Yarmouth at dawn on Sunday with no place to sleep. So we'd sleep under the pier, on the beach, waiting for them to open the theatre so we could get the gear in. It was pretty arduous stuff but we had a lot of fun doing this."

It was while on the road with Billy Fury that he heard his first jazz record: Duke Ellington at the 1956 Newport Jazz Festival with the classic track "Diminuendo and Crescendo in Blue", on which tenor saxophone player Paul Gonsalves takes countless choruses and the crowd goes nuts. "This was a jazz album," he says, "but I could identify with it because it was really kind of like rock 'n' roll. And there was a wonderful live recording by Peggy Lee called *Beauty and the Beat!* which was recorded in Miami, Florida in 1959. She was accompanied by the George Shearing Quintet: great songs, immaculate arrangements, and wonderful performances by Peggy Lee. And I heard Billie

Holiday and Ella Fitzgerald." His ears were opening up and he began following this serious music more deeply.

At the end of 1960 several groups were sent to Paris to play the Olympia theatre on a concert that was headlined by Chubby Checker, the "twist" man. The line-up was Chubby Checker, Billy Fury and the Blue Flames, the Shadows (without Cliff Richard) and Vince Taylor, an American rock 'n' roller who lived in London.

The first night in town, Georgie went to the Blue Note and heard the great American jazz pianist Bud Powell. Powell, aside from having the same last name as Georgie, was the Black American musician who revolutionized the bebop idiom of jazz, along with giants like Thelonious Monk and Charlie Parker. The place was almost empty. Georgie sat quietly in the back with a glass of wine. At a table near the bandstand, he noticed actor Robert Mitchum, surrounded by a bevy of beautiful girls, having a ball. Bud was all over the piano. It was a dramatic, iconic musical evening that stayed with him; there was a road leading into the jazz woods.

At the soundcheck the next day, in a totally empty theatre – not even Billy Fury was there – the musicians, rather than playing one of Billy's tunes, started messing around with a song called "In a Summer Place" which had been recorded by the Percy Faith Orchestra. All this new material was creeping into their consciousness and, since the point of a soundcheck was to test the gear and the sound system, it didn't seem like a problem to the musicians on stage.

But Hal Carter, the roadie, and Larry Parnes were at the back of the hall. As the band was working their way through the song, Hal came rushing down the aisle to the stage saying, "It's not rocking! It's not rocking!" "Course it wasn't," says Georgie, "We weren't playing one of Billy's tunes, we were playing something else. So we told him to get lost in no uncertain terms." After the concert, which was a great success, everybody went off to a trendy Parisian discotheque where Chubby Checker was going to give them a twist lesson.

They all returned to England and nothing more was said about the dust-up with Hal at the soundcheck in Paris. The next gig with Billy was a few weeks later (January 1961), in Boston in Lincolnshire, miles away from anywhere, at a venue called the Gliderdrome. The gig was on a Sunday, and the band hadn't been given any road transport, just one-way rail tickets to get to Boston from London with all their gear, the bass amp, drum kit and guitar amp – the usual things. Georgie says, "We boarded the train at King's Cross station for a journey that should have taken four hours. But there had been some kind of railway accident that day and our train was diverted all over the east of England and we didn't arrive at Boston until about ten o'clock that night. By then they'd closed the Gliderdrome, because there was no way Billy could have performed. He'd left with Hal Carter, the roadie, in the car. There was nobody there when we arrived and we were supposed to be paid that night and we were going to buy our return tickets back to London out of that money.

"Nobody had any money. We had nowhere to sleep and we spent the night in one of the rooms on the platform of Boston railway station, where a kindly night porter built us a big coal fire. We slept on the benches and the next morning we took the first train back to King's Cross, London. When the ticket collector came to our compartment, of course we didn't have any tickets, but fortunately one or two of us had our passports because we'd just returned from Paris. He accepted our story that we'd been delayed the previous day and couldn't get to our workplace and so we hadn't been paid. I think there was some kind of agreement that, within a month, we could pay our ticket in arrears and there wouldn't be any problem.

"And that was the last gig we ever did with Billy Fury. We all got the sack after that. It wasn't Billy that fired us. He would never have fired us. He was a great guy, Billy. It was Hal Carter, the roadie, who had a lot to do with it.

"But no offence to any of them. It was all wonderful experience – on the road with Larry Parnes."

3 The Flamingo

> **"We went in and that was it. We stayed for three years. We found our home – our spiritual home."**

All the other musicians besides Georgie were London-based so, when they got the sack from Billy, they had families and homes to go to. Georgie had nothing but a bit of money in the bank. He'd given up his room in Islington with the Greek Cypriot family. So he went back to Leigh to wait and see. But the only job offer that came along was with Tommy Steele's younger brother, Colin Hicks, who was trying to make a name for himself as a singer with the Cabin Boys . He offered the whole Bill Fury band a job in Egypt, of all places, but the job never materialized.

After a couple of weeks, with his family gradually digesting the bad news of his being fired from the Parnes organization, Georgie decided to return to London and fall back on his friend Mike O'Neill. Nero and the Gladiators still had quite a lot of work up and down the country and Mike and Boots had an apartment in Soho at 33 Old Compton Street. Mike very kindly agreed to put Georgie up as long as he needed shelter. Most of the time Georgie slept on the floor, but if the boys were out on a gig he could sleep on one of the beds. It was a pretty small flat and, from mid-January to the middle of March 1962, that was his London home.

He didn't have his own set of keys for the flat and had to be careful about when he went out and how long he stayed because, if the others were at a gig somewhere, hours from London, he could be locked out of the flat until they returned. More than once he wandered the streets of London until three in the morning when they returned. He'd go into a telephone box, put in his tuppence and call to see if anybody was home yet.

During this two-month stay in the apartment, Georgie absorbed Mike's small but thorough jazz record collection. He was quite happy to stay in the flat when the others were out working – sometimes not even worrying about food. One album that completely captured his imagination was *Chet Baker*

Sings with the trumpet player singing all these wonderful standards accompanied by Kenny Drew on piano. There was also the milestone recording by Lambert, Hendricks & Ross called *Sing a Song of Basie*, for which Jon Hendricks had written lyrics to Count Basie arrangements, including all the solos, and on which Jon, Annie Ross and Dave Lambert subsequently sang all the horn parts. It was brilliant lyric writing and one of the first examples of multi-tracked overdubbed vocals.

There was a Charlie Parker album, an album by Thelonious Monk with Art Blakey and the Jazz Messengers, and a fantastic recording by the Cannonball Adderley Quintet, *Them Dirty Blues*, which had "Work Song" on it. About this time, Boots Slade popped up with a vocal album by Oscar Brown Jr called *Sin & Soul* on which Oscar Brown sang lyrics he had written to "Work Song". This was a revelation to Georgie: you could write lyrics to instrumentals and even solos. So it was all coming together for him: jazz, vocals and great-grooved American music. And, finally, there was a duet by vocalist King Pleasure with Jon Hendricks on the Stan Getz composition "Don't Get Scared", a major moment in the art of "vocalese": sophisticated lyrics written to jazz solos.

He was listening to all this new, amazing music. He could *hear* a Charlie Parker chorus being played, but a lot of it was going over his head, intellectually. But when he listened to Jon Hendricks or King Pleasure singing the same Charlie Parker solo – with text – it all made sense. He spent two months absorbing this musical revolution in Mike's flat.

Mike knew about a jazz club just around the corner in Wardour Street, where they had all-night sessions on Fridays and Saturdays, midnight till 6 am. It was called the Flamingo and he took Georgie down there one night after midnight and introduced him to the man running the place, a charismatic, colourful character called Rik Gunnell.

Eric Clapton says in the Martin Scorsese documentary *Nothing But the Blues* that, when he first went down to the Flamingo, he was terrified because it was so dark in there. By "dark" he didn't just mean with no lights but because most of the audience was Black. When Georgie went down there that first night, into this dark, hot, steamy room, after his eyes had adjusted to the shadowy atmosphere he saw three or four rows of chairs immediately in front of the bandstand and most of the action going on in the back – people dancing, people wandering around, a little coffee bar over here and a Coca-Cola bar back there. It was just a scene.

"I was totally in awe," says Georgie, "because it was mainly frequented by Black American GIs who were stationed in the United States Air Force in England. And on weekends they would all pile into London's Soho, and the Flamingo club was their home because of the all-night sessions. The club was jammed with West Indians, a few Africans, pimps, prostitutes, small-time gangsters, lots of showgirls who worked in the society clubs in Bond Street, where the aristocracy and Members of Parliament would meet; when they'd finished their work at three o'clock in the morning, they would all head down to the Flamingo because it was still jumping till 6 am."

The next week, he and Mike went back into the all-nighter. Rik Gunnell told them that the rock 'n' roll house band, Earl Watson and the Chevingtons, had to go up to Birmingham to do some kind of television recording. He needed a band to "dep" – to fill in – so Mike and Georgie started talking fast. "We said, 'Well, look, we've got a band – we've got a four-piece band. We just played with Billy Fury for two years, and, you know, we can do it.' And Rik Gunnell said, 'Okay, you're in. You start at three o'clock next Sunday afternoon. You play from three to six with a break.'

"We went in and that was it. We stayed for three years. We found our home – our spiritual home, really. And it was thanks to Mike O'Neill that I secured this residency. Then my whole musical education opened up because we were allowed to play the kind of music that we'd heard on records but hadn't been allowed to play with Larry Parnes. We'd heard Ray Charles, Oscar Brown Jr, King Pleasure, Louis Prima – at that stage I hadn't heard the great Louis Jordan and the Timpani Five, I was just hip to Louis Prima – so we started to play all this stuff. We would rehearse new material all the time and pile it all in. We played three one-hour sets a night and it just got better and better.

"The GIs loved us. I can remember a GI named Carl Smith, from Grand Rapids, Michigan who was stationed at Newbury Air Force base – Smitty, as we called him. One weekend he came down to the club and said, 'Hey Georgie, you ever heard of Mose Allison?' I said, 'No man.' And the next weekend he came down with a couple of Mose Allison records because he was a big fan of Mose. And I fell in love with Mose Allison – started to buy all his records and tried to start sounding like him. Another Black American GI whose name was George Conley, from Chicago, was stationed out in Suffolk. He was another loner. He didn't come down team-handed as some of them did. He was on his own. He'd heard me sing some of this King Pleasure stuff on stage at the Flamingo and we got talking in the break and Conley said to me, 'Hey have you ever heard of Eddie Jefferson?' And I said, 'No man.' Next weekend he brought me an Eddie Jefferson album. Eddie Jefferson was another of these wonderful vocalese singers that put lyrics to great bebop players' solos and sang them. So that's how my musical education progressed.

"Sometimes these GIs would come over to Mike's apartment and hang out after we'd finished playing at 6 am. Or we'd all come back to my flat and we would play music and talk until midday and then get some sleep before we had to go back to work in the evening." Georgie was absorbing jazz and American rhythm and blues, drinking it in like water, and it arrived just on time as, remarkably, he had both the thirst for musical knowledge and the innate ability to understand and sing it.

The regular British jazz group that played opposite the Blue Flames on Friday all-nighters was the Johnny Burch Quartet. Burch was a fine jazz piano player, and he had Dick Heckstall-Smith on tenor saxophone, Jack Bruce on string bass and Ginger Baker on drums (the latter two the future rhythm section of the rock group Cream). Alexis Korner, among others, would come down to the Flamingo after finishing work to hang out and listen to the bands. The club was a hotbed for the coming British blues scene.

Rik Gunnell didn't own the club; he just ran the all-night sessions. The club was owned by the Kruger brothers, who didn't care much for rock 'n' roll. They had a baby grand piano but it was reserved for jazz musicians only – Georgie wasn't allowed to play it because he was playing rhythm and blues. So he had to rent an upright piano, which he played for several months, until another option appeared on the scene.

One of his friends was a Jamaican disc jockey by the name of Count Suckle. "Suckle had a wonderful sound system," he remembers, "as lots of the Jamaicans had, with big, big speakers. He also had a great source of recorded material: he knew someone in Memphis, Tennessee who used to send him all the latest soul and blues from America. And of course Suckle, being West Indian, had all the great bluebeat and traditional Jamaican and West Indian music.

"Suckle was looking for a club of his own. There was a property in Carnaby Street, before Carnaby Street became the big fashion street, and Suckle had the opportunity to take over this room, which he did. He opened it with an all-night session on a Sunday and we were the band that played opposite his sound system (a hopeless task because the sound system was fantastic, and we were just a little band having to play).

"Suckle had this wonderful record collection and that's where I first heard James Brown's 'Night Train' and Booker T. & the M.G.'s playing 'Green Onions'. Before the people came in at midnight, while there was only staff in the club and everything was being set up, Suckle would play these and other wonderful Blue Note recordings on this big sound system and we'd all dance around until the public came in. Coincidently, I'd heard *Midnight Special* by Jimmy Smith with Stanley Turrentine on saxophone, in the Flamingo during the breaks. They also used to play a great live recording by the Chicago tenor saxophonist Gene Ammons. It was called *Groovin' with Jug*, and Gene Ammons was accompanied by Richard "Groove" Holmes. And all these records featured the Hammond organ.

"I heard all this music in the same week and I decided, after struggling with this upright piano in the Flamingo for several months, to buy my first Hammond organ. I bought a Hammond L100, which was a spinet model. It didn't have the full range of the Hammond B3 keyboard but it did have the Hammond sound. And that kind of revolutionized the sound of the band.

"When we first started playing the Flamingo we actually accompanied the saxophone player Earl Watson. We became his backing band, and I also started to do a lot of singing, a lot more than I had been doing. But Earl, for some reason, after a few weeks, started getting a bit bolshie. I don't know – he was a bit of a hard taskmaster. I wouldn't like to say that he got a bit too big for his boots, but he started to push us around a little bit. He went to Rik

Gunnell and started to whinge about something or other and he tried to get us fired. And Rik turned around and said, 'No. *You're* fired.'

"So we were left with the Blue Flames as a quartet, without a saxophone player. Fortunately, Rik had an old friend – his name was Mick Eve – who became a great influence on the development of the Blue Flames and was the Blue Flames' first tenor player. Mick joined the band on tenor saxophone and brought in a baritone saxophone player that he knew, a man by the name of Johnny Marshall who was considerably older than the rest of us and had played in the better British dance bands. A great baritone player.

"Suddenly the band was Hammond organ, guitar, electric bass (Tex Makins had become the Blue Flames' bass player), Red Reece on drums and two saxophone players. We were going from strength to strength. Mick would arrange rehearsals at least one day a week and we'd come in with all this new material, stuff that we managed to collect from Count Suckle's collection as well as all the latest Tamla Motown stuff and all the latest soul recordings from America. These were not generally available in 1962 in the shops in England and came to us through the black American GIs who arrived at the club with their car boots full of bourbon and records. We had amazing access to this music we wanted to play and this lifestyle that we wanted to live."

With the new line-up, the band became Georgie Fame and the Blue Flames. Then things started to happen quickly. They were packing the place out on the Friday and Saturday all-nighters opposite these great British jazz groups. And they played Sunday afternoon sessions from three till six for the stragglers, particularly the Americans that couldn't get back to base until later in the day.

A lot of interesting and unusual people started coming down to the gig. "There was one particular man who was very influential," remembers Georgie. "His name was Ronan O'Rahilly – an Irishman with the gift of the gab – a very pleasant character. Ronan had great foresight, and actually was responsible for starting the first pirate radio station in England, Radio Caroline. I used to go to his apartment in London and he had a huge map on the floor with architectural drawings of this big ship that he'd acquired. I think it was parked up in some Norwegian fjord. And he said, 'You see this boat? I'm going to take it to my grandfather's port in Greenore in Ireland, in the Republic just south of the border with Ulster.' He said, 'We're going to kit it out, put disc jockey decks on it and I'm going to park it in the North Sea and we're going to beam all our favourite music which the BBC and other radio stations are not playing so that the great British public can hear what's going on.'

"Everybody went, 'This guy is crazy!' But, of course, he did it. And Rik Gunnell, who was paying us, was party to all this. And then Rik suddenly started thinking, 'Well if there's all this interest in this band and they're packing my club out, if anything happens and I lose the band ... I better become a manager.' He had no aspirations to become a musical or theatrical manager: he was quite happy running the club and making a lot of money because it was packed for every session. But Rik decided he had to become a manager."

More importantly, Rik decided he had to become *Georgie's* manager. Georgie was still underage – he was 19 and couldn't sign a legal contract until he was 21 – so Rik drove Georgie to Lancashire, to his parents' home, where his father signed the management contract on Georgie's behalf.

Rik opened an office at 47 Gerrard Street – the Rik Gunnell Agency – where, coincidentally, a couple of years previously Georgie had gone into the basement to do the first musical rehearsal with Eddie Cochran and Gene Vincent. Suddenly, all these other bands started appearing on the scene. Apart from playing opposite the Johnny Burch Quartet, Georgie was now trading sets with the Tubby Hayes Quartet, the Tommy Whittle Quartet (at that time with Brian Auger playing piano) and the Don Rendell Quintet with Ian Carr on trumpet.

It was a fantastic musical education which the boys were absorbing at a rapid rate – and enjoying the hell out of it playing all night long. And they were meeting all these wonderful characters and rubbing shoulders with some great musicians. It was a dream come true. Chris Farlowe and the Thunderbirds played a lot down at the Flamingo with Albert Lee on guitar. And John Mayall used to come down from Manchester at weekends to hang out at the club and get up and jam a little, before he moved to London and formed John Mayall and the Bluesbreakers. John always had great guitar players in his band, including Eric Clapton, and they played frequently down at the Flamingo all-nighter as well. One particular band that was a favourite of Georgie's was led by a man from Bournemouth by the name of George "Zoot" Money – Zoot Money's Big Roll Band. They eventually took over the residency at the Flamingo when the Blue Flames started to make hit records. "I thought that Zoot always had by far the best British R&B band at that time," says Georgie. "It was a tight disciplined unit and they played great."

During this early period, the personnel in the Blue Flames was changing regularly. Red Reece was a great swinging drummer but, unfortunately, he started to dabble in drugs and became incapable of doing the gig. They then called on Jimmie Nicol, who was a great drummer from the Larry Parnes days, to join the band. The Beatles used to come down to the all-nighters, and one night, in 1963, Ringo was struck down with appendicitis, just as the Beatles were about to start a Far Eastern/Australian tour. Jimmie had only been in the Blue Flames a short time when Georgie got a call from the Beatles' office saying, "Ringo's sick: we need a drummer. Can we use your drummer, Jimmie Nicol?" The boys had heard him playing in the club.

Jimmie went off with the Beatles to play in Singapore and elsewhere before Ringo was well enough to join the tour. He came back to London with a swollen head because he'd done a few stadium gigs with the Beatles and he didn't want to go back to playing in the all-nighter with Georgie Fame and the Blue Flames. He wanted to form his own band, which he did: Jimmie Nicol and the Shubdubs. It went nowhere.

Then Colin Green, a founding member of the Blue Flames and one of Georgie's musical mentors, had to leave for domestic reasons. Unlike the rest of the band, Colin was married, and the band had a pretty hard lifestyle. Colin needed more stability. Mick Eve, the saxophone player, who was really the de facto manager of the band – arranging rehearsals and looking after details because of his administrative skills – knew of a guitar player who could take Colin's place. His name was John McLaughlin. John joined the band and stayed for several months. With a jazz master like John in the band, a whole new world of music opened up.

And with Georgie playing Hammond organ, the band sounded unlike any other on the scene. And they were now working Friday evening sessions outside London in R&B clubs like the Ricky-Tick in Windsor and the Blue Moon Club at Hayes in Middlesex. They were also playing American Air Force bases on Fridays and Saturdays because the GIs who came down to the Flamingo would recommend them to their entertainment bookers.

"I can remember we played at Chicksands Air Force base, in Cambridgeshire," says Georgie, "where a large proportion of the GIs who came down to the all-nighter were from. They fixed a night for Georgie Fame and the Blue Flames to play in their airmen's club and the place was packed. There were probably only three or four white guys in there, not including us. The place was full of our Flamingo brothers, and we were all having a ball.

"We would play these gigs on a Friday or Saturday until ten, 11 in the evening, come offstage, pack the gear in the wagon, drive back to London from wherever we were and continue playing at the all-night sessions at the Flamingo, which started at midnight with one of the great British jazz groups. So we really didn't have to be there, on stage, until 1 am. We would alternate sets until six o'clock in the morning. Then we'd play the Sunday-afternoon session for the stragglers, and an early Sunday-evening session in some little club in Jermyn Street or maybe up in Finchley Road till 11 o'clock, and then we'd go into Carnaby Street to play the all-nighter at Suckle's, the Jamaican all-nighter, till six o'clock Monday morning. So from Friday evening until Monday morning we were playing music, hauling gear, and playing more music. It was getting pretty hectic but we didn't know better. We were having a great time, learning more all the time."

With all this action, Rik Gunnell decided that he should open the Flamingo on Tuesday and Thursday evenings because the demand was so high. So all these other bands started appearing at the club. Early one Thursday evening in 1963, the Rolling Stones were playing in the Flamingo club and Georgie went down with John McLaughlin to check it out. The place was practically empty. There was a handful of West Indian guys wandering around and that was it. The Stones had built their reputation down in Richmond, in Surrey, where they had a huge fan base, and perhaps they played in a couple of other clubs in the West End, but the Flamingo was such a special kind of place that the Stones' fans didn't follow them there. It was bizarre, says Georgie, to listen to the Rolling Stones play in an empty room.

Perhaps the moment of the club's greatest infamy came during the so-called Profumo Affair, which had its origins at the Flamingo. John Profumo, the Secretary of State for War in Harold Macmillan's Conservative government, had a brief affair with a would-be model named Christine Keeler. When the Profumo–Keeler affair was first revealed, public interest was piqued by reports that Keeler may have also been involved at the same time with a Soviet naval attaché named Ivanov. Keeler knew both Profumo and Ivanov through her friendship with an osteopath and socialite named Stephen Ward, who had provided her a place to stay and taken her to important social affairs and introduced her around. The affair put a spotlight on Ward's other activities, and he was ultimately charged with a series of immorality offences. He took a fatal overdose during the final stages of his trial, which ultimately found him guilty of living off the immoral earnings of Keeler.

The way the affair came to light, however, was through a dispute that broke out at the Flamingo all-nighter. "There were two Jamaican guys," says Georgie, "one was called Johnny Edgecombe who was always known as Johnny Shit, maybe because he was dealing grass. And there was another guy known as Lucky Gordon. They used to fight over Christine Keeler when she came into the club with Zoot Money's future wife. They were both club girls, and when they'd finish working Bond Street in these society clubs, at 3 am on a Friday and Saturday, they'd come straight down to Wardour Street and make the last three hours of the session in the club.

"They'd come in to party, dancing on the tables and all that. Christine was involved with Johnny Edgecombe and there was a scene one night where Johnny Edgecombe cut Lucky Gordon with a knife down at the Flamingo over Christine. Then, a few weeks later, when the Flamingo was closed at 6 am, on a Friday or Saturday, Johnny Edgecombe went around to the flat where Christine was staying – she was sharing it with this homosexual osteopath named Ward – and Johnny popped off a couple of shots outside. In those days, there were no guns in London. Johnny was calling up to her, 'You *raas claat*. Come down here man. Talk to me when I talk to you.' And she said, 'Fuck you anyway.' So, *bang bang*, he fires off a couple of shots.

"The police came around and they investigated it and it all got exposed. How come this guy has got this gun in this street and he's dealing with this showgirl who is sharing this arrangement with the homosexual osteopath who had aristocratic connections, who used to take her to Lord Astor's house outside of London where Profumo was known to be, and there's a Russian naval attaché there as well? And it's all because Johnny Edgecombe went *bang bang*. It was great. It set off this huge investigation. We were all laughing about it."

Photo 7: Georgie with the Blue Flames: Mick Eve, Speedy Acquaye, Red Reece, Johnny Marshall, Tex Makins.

Courtesy James Powell

It was time for Georgie Fame and the Blue Flames to start making records: their audience and their reputation was growing daily. But the record companies then, as now, were unaware of what was happening below the surface, on the streets. So in 1963, after several approaches were made to major record companies, Rik Gunnell decided to put the money up himself and record the group's first LP, *Rhythm and Blues at the Flamingo*.

They did it one afternoon in front of a crowd of invited regulars. By this time the band had acquired a conga drummer from Ghana by the name of Neemoi Acquaye, known as Speedy. Speedy was a regular at the Flamingo. He used to walk in with his conga drum and sit in with the various bands, and he became a regular with the Blue Flames. Coming from Africa, he enjoyed a smoke of the natural weed and, on occasion, he'd come into the dressing room, turn the drum over and out would fall a nice bag of herb. Unfortunately, he got busted and, because it wasn't his first offence, received a two-month prison sentence.

Georgie went to visit him in Pentonville Prison. "It was very sad to see him cooped up like that," he says, "for something which he regarded as totally natural and normal. He'd being doing it all his adult life. Rumour has it that he actually said to the magistrate, when asked if he had anything to say, 'My mother used to put it in my tea.'"

Because he was detained at Her Majesty's pleasure, Speedy couldn't be there when the band recorded at the Flamingo, so a West Indian guy called Tommy Thomas who hung out at the club and played bongo drums filled in. Bongos, being a totally different instrument with a much higher register, changed the sound of the band.

Rik Gunnell had brought in a professional record producer by the name of Ian Samwell – "Sammy", as he was known. Sammy had composed Cliff Richard's first big hit "Move It" ("C'mon pretty baby, let's a move it and a groove it") from which he had made quite a lot of money and acquired a good reputation as a producer. But he hadn't really spent any time in the Flamingo club. It was a totally alien scene to him.

This was in September 1963, and John McLaughlin had just left the band. Georgie felt they'd been working fine with two saxophones, Speedy on the congas, Hammond organ, guitar, bass and drums, but Sammy, as a producer, thought a guitar player was required. The only guitar player Georgie could think of was Jim Sullivan, who had played with Marty Wilde's band back in the Larry Parnes days. Jim was doing a lot of session work by that time and wasn't really living the band lifestyle, but they called him and he too was thrown into the Blue Flames. So with Jim on guitar and Tommy Thomas on bongo drums, the whole sound of the band changed for the recording.

The engineer that had been booked was Glyn Johns, one of Britain's most successful recording engineers. Glyn had rented a two-track mobile unit from Chris Blackwell at Island Records. Chris had recently returned from Jamaica in 1962 having set up Island there, with dreams of creating one of the largest independent recording companies. But the operation at the Flamingo was bootstrap at best. Looking at the stage, to the left was a little band room, and on the other side was a small rat-infested room, used as a broom cupboard for the cleaners' equipment and whatnot. That was where Glyn decided to install the recording gear.

On the day of the gig, the place was packed. Everybody was primed to have a good time. The programme was all worked out. Glyn started the recording, and the band launched into a smoking set that lasted for the better part of an hour. It sounded good on the stage and the audience was having a ball. After the set, all the musicians streamed into the little room where Glyn was sitting with his headphones on, asking, "How does it sound? How is it?" Glyn told them, "I'm sorry, one of the tracks went down and didn't record. You'll have go and to do it *all* over again."

So they went back and re-recorded the whole thing again. The music that made it on the album was not the ferocious first take, but it *was* their first recording – a Rik Gunnell Independent Production – and suddenly, they were a recording band. Ultimately, Rik did a deal with EMI where they took the

Photo 8: At the Twisted Wheel, Manchester, 1964.
Courtesy James Powell

recording and provided financing to record further material, but all the rights eventually reverted back to Rik. He was way ahead of the game: although the licensing of independent recordings to major labels had been around since the mid-1950s, it would be years before it became usual rock 'n' roll business practice.

The record was treated as an instant classic and, seemingly overnight, the Blue Flames were in great demand. They hadn't had any hits but they did have a big popular following and were now playing clubs as far afield as Manchester. There was a great all-nighter club there called the Twisted Wheel, where the Blue Flames would start at midnight and go on until 6 am. When they were up in Manchester, other bands like Zoot Money, Chris Farlowe or John Mayall would do the Flamingo all-nighters.

Things started rolling, gigs were coming in and the pay was rising. "I clearly remember the first 50-quid gig we got," says Georgie, "which was actually on the east coast of England in Cleethorpes. We were so excited that the band was being paid £50 for one gig in a club that we drove all the way to Cleethorpes, did the gig, and then drove back to London and played half the all-nighter, just to celebrate.

"We did the same thing from that infamous place in Boston where I lost my gig with Billy Fury. The Blue Flames played the Gliderdrome and then drove back to London and got to the all-nighter at two o'clock in the morning, set up the gear on the stage – the other band had been playing – and off we went. That was typical of our working week in those days. We were doing ten gigs a week – ten different places in a seven-day week – for quite a while.

"There was a guy who would turn up at the coffee bar in the Flamingo who was known as Peter the Pill. And we'd get our weekly supply of little blues or something, whatever they were, to keep us awake, which we didn't take all the time but we took whenever we needed to. So we never really had bad gigs down at the Flamingo."

However, by the summer of 1963, the long late nights were starting to get to him and Georgie was looking more than a bit knackered. Rik had an old girlfriend who owned a motel down in Cornwall, in Redruth, and it was decided that Georgie should be sent away for a week to recuperate and get some rest. Brian Auger took a sabbatical from Tommy Whittle's quartet and played with the Blue Flames while Georgie went south for some R&R.

"I took the train all the way down to Cornwall," he says, "which is a very pleasant, relaxing ride, took a bus down to Redruth, got off at the bus stop outside the motel and checked in with a very nice lady, this friend of my manager, who welcomed me.

"The second morning I decided to take a bus to St Ives, a very pleasant Cornish resort. It was a boiling hot day. I walked to the beach and, taking a leaf out of my father's book, who used to park himself in the back yard at home in Lancashire and put olive oil on his face and get a bit of a sun tan, I put olive oil on my face and my body and lay down on the beach, fell asleep, woke up an hour later and I couldn't move.

"I had really bad sunstroke. With the weak sun that you would get up in Lancashire, it wasn't a problem. But there in Cornwall, I got seriously burned. I hauled myself off the beach, staggered back to the bus stop, freezing cold, shivering in the shade and in the sun, burning, on fire, and took a bus back to the hotel. I told them I wasn't feeling too good and one of the ladies who worked there came to my room and bathed me in chamomile lotion to try and save my skin and reduce my temperature.

"Things went from bad to worse. By the early evening I was feeling so ill I couldn't walk. I fell out of bed and crawled along the corridor to the reception area where there was a party going on. I crawled in on my hands and knees and said, 'I'm dying, you've got to do something.' They called an ambulance and took me to Truro Hospital where I spent ten days recovering from severe sunstroke.

"When I arrived, I had a temperature of 106 degrees, which I think might be one short of dead. And that was my holiday. Ten days later I was feeling fit enough to return back to London and rejoin the fray."

In his absence, while Brian Auger was depping, Red Reece had been making moves to stop Georgie from rejoining the band because he liked Brian Auger's playing so much. But, in the end, the band said goodbye to Red because of his problems with drugs and a succession of drummers followed.

One of them was the jazz drummer Phil Seamen. Phil was a heavy junkie. "Once you see what they have to do to maintain their habit," says Georgie, "you'll never do it. You'll never get that far gone. Phil used to say, 'If I ever catch you doing this, I'll fucking beat the shit out of you.' But he knew his music." Everybody did their turn looking after Phil, and some of them, unfortunately, ended up in trouble themselves. But even if Phil "looked like a sack of shit" when he got on the bandstand, he almost always played wonderfully.

Phil had a deep knowledge of the music and the lifestyle and a great ability to share it with the others. Even now, some people would say he was the greatest jazz drummer that Britain ever produced because of his flair for "the real swing". And he could explain the difference between Art Blakey and Buddy Rich and Philly Joe Jones, and the difference between the suave approach of Duke Ellington and the free-spirited blues of Count Basie, to the others even while they were actually looking after him.

One day, Phil said to Georgie, "Oh, by the way, Chet's coming around." A couple of hours later, there was a knock at the door and Chet Baker, clearly unwell, was standing there. He had just arrived in London and was looking to score heroin. Georgie took one look at him and said, "Come on in. Phil's in the back kitchen" and sat back down in the little front room while the legendary American musician did his business with Phil. About 45 minutes later, Georgie heard the door slam and Phil came into the living room and said, "Jesus, I thought *I* was heavy..." It was Georgie's first introduction to a man who would become one of his main inspirations.

Phil *was* a heavy user. Once, in Manchester, at the Twisted Wheel, the band started the midnight session, played the whole set, and Phil, who was sitting at the drum kit, never hit the drums. He nodded through the whole set. All these young kids in the room were going, "What's going on? The band's playing and nothing's happening with the drummer." He had obviously taken too many Nembutals, which were the heavy sleeping pills he took when he didn't have access to heroin. He just nodded his way through the whole thing.

You can't continue like that. But, Georgie says, "He was a great person, a wonderful person, and when you sit with these people from another generation, they *know*. They can give you all the information you want, if you're prepared to listen." The trick is get the information before you too become part of the information.

In 1964, Georgie knew it was time for a change; he had to get somebody younger in the band, a drummer that could do the gig physically as well as

Photo 9: The Blue Flames: Georgie (front left) with Mitch Mitchell. Back row: Peter Coe, Colin Green, Cliff Barton and Eddie Thornton.

Courtesy James Powell

musically. Phil sat in as Georgie auditioned two new candidates, Micky Waller and Mitch Mitchell. Each one came on and played a couple of tunes with the band while Phil sat in the audience and applied his critical ear to the music. They knew who he was and were most certainly intimidated. In the end, Phil said, "Yeah, Mitch probably tops it a little bit over the other guy", and that was it: Mitch Mitchell had the gig.

It was the beginning of the greatest period down at the Flamingo, with a stream of American musicians coming down and sitting in with the band. The legendary trumpet player Thad Jones, when he was touring with Count Basie's orchestra in England, came down to the Flamingo all-nighter with his horn and played the blues with the Blue Flames, rather than joining the jazz group that was playing opposite that night. The same thing happened with Cat Anderson, Duke Ellington's lead trumpet player. And Babs Gonzales, the wild jazz rapper from New York, came down and hung out with the band whenever he was in town. One night, on his first tour of the UK, along with Gene McDaniels and Johnny Burnett, even Gary U.S. Bonds came to the Flamingo all-nighter and got up on the stage to perform his big hit "New Orleans".

Some of the regular GIs were also very good singers. One, named Ronnie Jones from Boston, Massachusetts, was stationed at High Wycombe Air Force base. He had a great singing voice and would get up and sing the Joe Williams/Count Basie hit "Every Day I Have the Blues" and a couple of other tunes. Geno Washington was another American serviceman, based at Bentwaters, out in Suffolk, who used to come down to the club every weekend and sing with the band. At the end of their service careers, both of these men went back to the States, mustered out of the US Air Force, and then came straight back to England where they established themselves in successful singing careers.

Because of the rising interest in their music, some of the greatest American blues singers were starting to come over to England as well – singers like John Lee Hooker, Sonny Boy Williamson and Memphis Slim. They too made their way down to the Flamingo and wound up performing, and occasionally touring, with the Blue Flames.

"We had backed Sonny Boy Williamson in the south of England," remembers Georgie, "and one night he turned up at the Flamingo all-nighter. He had this checked suit on, with the joker's squares, which was his trademark. And he was drunk. Very drunk. He came into the band room while we were on our break and basically put me up against the wall. He stuck his face in my face and said, 'Boy, can you write a song about this suit?' I didn't really know what he was talking about. At the time, I couldn't write a song about anything let alone his suit. I didn't quite get his drift. I knew there was an undercurrent of threat there. Phil Seamen was in the band room at the time, and Phil grabbed hold of Sonny Boy Williamson and said, 'Don't mess with this boy', and threw him out of the room. He didn't come back."

A couple of years later, Muddy Waters came to England to record an album with a selection of British players. It was to be called *The London Muddy Waters Sessions* and Georgie was one of the players called to IBC Studios to record with him. "Jimmy Page was there," says Georgie, "and also Rory Gallagher. There wasn't an organ so I played the piano. Muddy was just sitting there, not in the soundproof booth but in amongst the band with a microphone in front of him, just like the old days. Everything he played was in F sharp or B natural and I'm having a terrible time. Even though it's just simple Chicago, Delta blues, whatever you want to call it, these were tough keys for a piano player. The guitar players are all cool, of course, but I'm on eggshells because you don't want to play that note if you're not sure it's gonna be right, because you've never been there before. You're treading on a landmine.

"So I thought I was stiff and not really very good. About a year later, after the album came out, I met Muddy Waters somewhere, and of course he was a sweet guy, perfect gentleman. I said, 'I'm terribly sorry Muddy. I played on half of that album, and I really wasn't comfortable because everything you played was either in the key of F sharp or B natural, and those are keys I've never played in before or since.' And he said, 'Shit man, you should have told me. I would have just moved the capo.'

"But when you've been invited to play with God in the studio, you're not going to say, 'Hey man, it's the wrong key. Do you mind shifting a semitone one way or the other and I'll be cool.' But that's what he said to me. 'You should have told me, I would have moved the capo.' That's what the gentlemen are like: easy-going, no sweat. He was the opposite to what Sonny Boy Williamson was like."

It went on like this for months down at the Flamingo, with Georgie receiving a priceless tuition nightly. The accolades of elder statesmen and the advice from hardcore jazz musicians was invaluable schooling. "We were just these young whippersnappers, and they'd walk on the bandstand and say, 'Yeah man, yeah,' while we're playing; you know: 'You're doing something right so keep doing it.'"

Finally, Ronan O'Rahilly, who was about to launch Radio Caroline, opened his own club in Soho at the back of Great Windmill Street, in a little space called Ham Yard. He called it the Scene Club, and Georgie Fame and the Blue Flames opened it. It, too, went on to become a very successful British R&B venue.

A few days later Ronan came into the Flamingo and said, "Look, I've heard this fantastic band up in Newcastle. I'm going to bring them down and they're going to play in my Scene Club." The band was the Animals. Some time later, Georgie went around the corner on his break one night and there were the Animals in full flow. He remembers Eric Burdon was singing "Big Boss Man". "It was one of the best things I'd ever heard. Eric was jumping up and down on top of a beat-up old grand piano, which Alan Price, the pianist, wasn't playing – he was playing the Vox Continental, getting that unique British R&B sound – and it was really happening. It was raucous and raw, with a lot of real excitement and energy. We all introduced ourselves in the break and I went back to the Flamingo and carried on with my gig, but that was the start of my relationship with the Animals and particularly with Alan Price."

One Friday, the Blue Flames played an evening session at the Scene Club before they went to the all-nighter at the Flamingo. The English barrow boys in Berwick Street Market used to park their barrows overnight in Ham Yard. This evening, the band finished at the Scene at 11 o'clock, and had to get round into the Flamingo with their gear by midnight. But their van had broken down, so they took one of the barrows from the barrow park, piled all the equipment on it and pulled it all the way up Shaftesbury Avenue, through rush-hour traffic, up to Wardour Street, through the traffic lights – waiting for the green light, of course – and then pulled it around the corner to the Flamingo. When they got all the gear onstage, somebody took the barrow back to Ham Yard and parked it while the rest of the group carried on with the next gig. That's how things were happening: *non-stop!*

Easter Monday 1964 was the great dawning of Radio Caroline: the day it broadcast for the first time from the North Sea as a pirate radio station. The first three records that Caroline played were a Ray Charles tune, a Rolling Stones record and a cut from Georgie Fame and the Blue Flames' *Rhythm and Blues at the Flamingo*. Radio Caroline launched a whole new era in British broadcasting: after a couple of years the Labour government decided that they'd steal the pirates' thunder and set up Radio 1. All the disc jockeys who had been taking these little lighters out to the Radio Caroline boat suddenly found themselves land-based with jobs at the BBC.

It was a time of radio broadcast firsts, and Georgie was part of it. In 1964, the BBC decided to test the first stereo recording for broadcast. They chose an old theatre in Camden Town and both Georgie Fame and the Blue Flames and the Rolling Stones were selected to take part in the experiment. Clearly, it worked.

Several months later, the Blue Flames played the first "live remote" broadcast for the BBC. "It was at the Ricky-Tick in Windsor," says Georgie, "one of our favourite clubs. And we had two good friends, brothers: one was Keith Grant, a studio engineer at one of London's most famous studios in Barnes and his brother, Ian, who was a BBC producer. Ian was a great fan of the music and knew what was going on, and fought with the powers-that-be to get a live outside broadcast. Eventually, the BBC relented and the Blue Flames did the first-ever live outside broadcast from a club. That was another milestone because the BBC had never done any outside broadcasts from this new British R&B club scene. We were the first."

From the moment Ronan launched Radio Caroline, Georgie Fame and the Blue Flames were in heavy rotation. Naturally, the record company was keen for them to go into the studio to make more recordings. If they didn't have time to do an album, they would record EPs (extended plays): which were 45 rpm discs with four tracks, mini-albums with picture sleeves. The band would just pop into the recording studio for a couple of hours, as if they were doing a live gig, record four songs, pack up the gear and get off to the next gig. "The recording sessions used to interfere with our gig schedules," says Georgie, "because the gigs were the most important thing for us, playing live in the clubs. The recording scene was really a secondary thing. It hadn't yet got to the point where this huge recording industry blew up and swallowed up everything."

One evening, during one of his frequent visits to Ronan O'Rahilly's place, Georgie met the girl who would become his first serious relationship, both grounding him and challenging his perspective on what home life could be. Her name was Carmen Jimenez. "Carmen was very exotic," he says. "She looked and *was* Spanish, from Cataluña. I became quite besotted with her. We started a relationship almost immediately. Her parents had moved to England where she was actually born, but she spoke fluent Spanish. She was quite effusive and I was quite taken by her, and I pursued her. I suppose I was captivated by her."

At the time, he and two other musicians from the band were sharing a place in what were called "Rachman" accommodations. "There was a landlord by the name of Peter Rachman who was a pretty tough guy," says Georgie. "It was all very basic, cheap, so-called 'furnished accommodations'. On two or three occasions, we would come back from the all-nighter at the Flamingo and discover a piece of paper nailed to the door saying, 'Your belongings have been removed to such and such address' in another part of London. You'd go there and the key would be under the mat and that was your new flat."

With Carmen in the picture, Georgie wanted to rent his own place, away from the nightly crush. They were both living most days in the company of music and musicians. Carmen was very much a part of the club scene. "Actually," says Georgie, "she was a bit of an exhibitionist on the dance floor. I used to shy away from that kind of exhibitionism, but Mick Jagger loved dancing with her."

"We would all go around to these clubs together and eventually, when we started to make records, we would all hang out together in various clubs. The first place that we hung out in was on the top of a cinema in Leicester Square. I don't know the name of it but I remember it being one of the first places where me and the guys from other bands – the Rolling Stones, the Beatles, The Who – started to hang out. Where we could go and be ourselves.

"In those days, the favoured club lasted maybe three weeks for us because when the sycophants heard about the place, all of these other people started to invade the scene and we'd have to move on and find another place. So we were constantly on the move. That went on for months, and we found like five or six different clubs around central London where we could go and hang out and be semi-normal or just be ourselves.

"These were the little 'in' places – in fact, one of them was called the In Place – where we could be unbothered by punters, and just have each other's company. Carmen was always on the dance floor; she became a fixture on that scene. There was one place I remember called the Scotch of St James, which was a really good little club. I think that was probably our last place. We stopped moving after that."

It's remarkable how small the scene was at the time. The number of musicians recording classic Black American music or writing original versions of pop music and building a large young audience was probably numbered in the hundreds not thousands. It was like an extended family. Everybody knew everybody, and everybody was making it up at as they went along: musicians, managers, DJs, record companies. They were in uncharted waters and it was floating many more boats than just the *Caroline*. In a few years the business would abandon its children, so to speak, and surrender to the lawyers and the conglomerates. But, for this brief moment, most of the "British Invasion" scene could fit into a pub in Leicester Square.

At the centre of this exploding scene was Black American music. "The Stones were 100% purists," says Georgie. "They were into the Chicago blues and that was that. Chuck Berry was also one of their heroes. But, generally, Brian Jones was the catalyst for a lot of that pure blues harmonica stuff, whereas the Beatles were a bit more sophisticated. They were into melodies and harmonies. McCartney said they did the Motown thing; they took those kinds of influences and turned it to their own advantage, into something original. Everybody loved and danced to all the Motown records, to 'Twist and Shout' or the Isley Brothers. One of my favourite dance records of all time was 'Road Runner' by Junior Walker. Or 'Shotgun'. Those were guaranteed to get me up at the clubs.

"It was all Black music. You couldn't get Blacker. Sometimes we even used to speak to each other in Black patois because we wanted to be as Black as possible. We figured it was the only way to make the music swing. The closer we could get to the Blackness, the more likely we were to get to the real swing of things. I remember Jimmie Nicol would go around and whisper to us, 'It's got to be Black, man.' And he was sincere about everything. It was the only way to think of it.

"To swing was the most important thing in life. We had to get that swing. It was Black, so we had to obtain that Blackness. One night, we were smoking and the bass player, who was a fairly deep thinker, suggested that we actually get the soot from the chimney and blacken our faces with it, to see what it felt like to *be* Black. And we did it. Just sat there, stoned, listening to the music, sort of stonedly convincing ourselves that we could feel Black.

"At the time, the greatest thing I had was the acceptance of the Black American GIs. They knew what I wanted to know, and in many ways were what I wanted to be like. They were already *there*. So when we're sitting in my little room after the Flamingo all nighters, me and a guy like Carl Smith, and he brings in a couple of Mose Allison records from the PX and we're sitting there, alone together, listening to Mose, we're like brothers. We're digging the same thing."

Even though there was a sizeable West Indian population in post-war Britain, the Black experience was only starting to come to the fore. America was like another planet. Even playing on an American Air Force base was like going to another planet, where they had all the facilities, the ice, the fridge, the food, the cold beers, the bourbon and cokes, the clothes. And when Black GIs would go down to the club, the musicians *had* it too.

It was all there. The GIs would just park the car on Wardour Street, open up the boot and there were cases of bourbon and piles and piles of vinyl. "They'd say, 'Hey, Fame, what'chu want?' That's when I decided the name Georgie Fame, which I had detested from the start, sounded okay. In fact, coming from a black American GI it sounded pretty good. 'Hey Fame, motherfucker, what's happening?!' I thought, 'Well okay!'"

The GIs would always be willing to help musicians carry their gear on nights when the band would get back late to the Flamingo from out-of-town gigs. The place would already be packed with the jazz band playing, like Tubby Hayes or any of the great British jazzmen, finishing the first set. The Blue Flames would roll in after midnight and start the second set around 1:15 am. They'd have the Hammond organ with them, and the GIs would clear the way for them and lift the gear onto the stage, because they knew they couldn't start the real party until the band started playing.

"There was such a great feeling in the room and a variety of stuff we would play. We never repeated ourselves," says Georgie. "It might have been 'Work Song' with Oscar Brown Jr's lyrics. Or it could have been a West Indian thing like 'Humpty Dumpty' or bluebeat nursery rhymes. It was just something to get them dancing. It could have been anything: 'Let the Good Times Roll' by Ray Charles, 'Shop Around' by Smokey Robinson. We always saved 'Symphony Sid' for whenever there was a spot of trouble. They'd put the lights on and we would stop what we were playing and go into 'Symphony Sid', which would keep everybody happy, and it usually quelled the dust-up very quickly. I told that to the director of the movie *Absolute Beginners* and he put it in the movie.

"Because we made friends with these guys, we were truly living *the life*. There was no ambiguity. Everybody was totally open. These guys appreciated the fact that they could come to a place in Soho that they could practically claim as their own and hang out all night and have a ball."

And because of the darkness of the Flamingo, there was no other club like it. It had its own sense of style. Georgie was wearing a Bermuda jacket, a buttoned-down collar and a knitted tie, "like 90% American, but doing it in London". The Mods, who would be given credit for a similar style a little later, never went into the Flamingo, at least not until the US Air Force authorities proscribed it in early '64. That's when a some GI or other picked a fight with another GI and got himself stabbed. The Air Force authorities took it as an opportunity to put the club off limits. Within a week, the Mods realized that the Black American guys weren't going in there anymore so it was safe for them. They started filling the place up and then it became the Mod Flamingo.

The Mods were part of the generation of young British kids who filled the dance floor on the *Ready Steady Go!* TV series and were the epitome of the new British youth at that time. It followed on the heels of the Teddy Boy era. Mods considered themselves cool because they wore Italian-style clothes, rode Vespa or Lamborghini motor scooters and dug soul music. In the early '60s, the Mods also really dug The Who, whose image captured the whole Mod aesthetic. Rockers were the old guard (taking their cues still from Bill Haley and *Blackboard Jungle*, which glorified American juvenile delinquents with their black leather jackets and D.A. haircuts); they weren't interested in the soul side of things. The Mods and Rockers used to have pitched battles, most memorably in Brighton, as depicted in the film *Quadrophenia*. It was like two totally different cultures.

Part of the reason the club scene started to change for Georgie was that the musical environment was expanding on all fronts. He was listening to Jon Hendricks singing with Count Basie, alongside other great singers who worked with big bands, and he gradually developed an interest in trying to sing with a big band himself. His baritone player, Johnny Marshall, who had some experience with British dance bands, recommended that he go and see Harry South.

South had a quartet with Dick Morrissey, the great British tenor saxophone player, which played at the Bull's Head, a pub in Barnes, on the Thames in southwest London, and already a famous jazz establishment. Georgie took the bus to Barnes, walked into the crowded pub and there was Dick Morrissey and the Harry South Quartet in full flow with Phil Bates on bass and Phil Seamen on the drums.

In the break, he walked over and introduced himself to Harry and said that Johnny Marshall had recommended him and that he had an interest in trying to sing with a big band. At the time, Harry had a well-regarded jazz orchestra, which only worked occasionally, mainly for BBC radio *Jazz Club* broadcasts. He took to the idea immediately, and soon he and Georgie were putting material together, working on arrangements at Harry's flat in Streatham, South London. When Harry got tired of writing, or bored, a visit to his local betting shop would ensue, to put something on the horses. One time, Harry said, "Let's go up to town. We'll go to Ronnie's." Ronnie Scott's was *the* jazz establishment in Soho and Harry was a regular there. This time, he said, "Blossom Dearie is playing."

Blossom was a quirky American jazz singer and pianist with a reputation as a hip insider's insider. At the club, they found a little table on the balcony side of things and Blossom came over. Harry introduced her to Georgie. They had a quick chat and that was it. They went back to Harry's Streatham flat and carried on working.

"That same week," says Georgie, "was the only time I ever played in the Marquee Club, another famous venue on Wardour Street. I did a concert there with Harry's big band, one of the first concerts we ever did together, and rumour had it that Blossom had come in to hear the gig. A few days later, I thought, 'Oh, Blossom's still playing at Ronnie's. I'll go and have a listen.' It was nice because she sang all of those obscure tunes that you've never heard in that wonderful voice. I went into Ronnie's, got a table close to the bandstand. I sat there on my own and a couple of tunes in, she started to sing this song she had just written about me. It was called 'Sweet Georgie Fame'. I crawled under the table with embarrassment really.

"It's a great tune. If it wasn't about me, I'd sing it myself. It's a jazz waltz and, over the years, a lot of people have recorded it. Tony Bennett recorded it in the late '60s – he changed the words "darling boy's brought me joy" to "groovy boy's brought me joy". She got a lot of publicity out of it, and actually it was great for my profile as well because she is such a respected musician. To this day, a lot of people know my name without ever actually having heard anything I do, because of the song."

The album he and Harry South ultimately recorded was called *Sound Venture,* and it featured some of the greatest British jazz musicians: Ronnie Scott himself and Tubby Hayes on saxophones, Jackie Sharpe and a great trumpet section, and Stan Tracey on the piano. They recorded four songs at Pye Studios, including three Count Basie titles with lyrics by Jon Hendricks – "Little Pony," "Down for the Count" and "Li'l Darlin'", the Neal Hefti composition. Then they had to wait 18 months until Georgie had enough money to complete the album. He was paying for it himself. If you wanted to sing jazz, all the rules of pop stardom needn't apply. Record companies were not interested and musicians often did it on their own just to make the music – and a bit of music history – happen.

Meanwhile, he was still gigging with the Blue Flames, and the band was working hard; it was taking its toll on the musicians and the personnel kept changing. Johnny Marshall, for one, was succumbing to his drug habit. One night when they were playing in Manchester at a Twisted Wheel all-nighter and staying in a bed and breakfast, Johnny had the withdrawals and was distinctly unwell. He left his room in a fairly hysterical state, desperately looking for drugs. He forced himself into the wrong room and was rummaging through the drawers with some fellow asleep in bed. The man woke up, thought he was being burgled, and whacked Marshall in the face and broke his jaw. So Johnny wasn't going to be playing saxophone for a few weeks. Mick Eve knew a very fine up-and-coming young baritone saxophone player called Glenn Hughes who took Johnny's place.

But then, one day, Mick was unceremoniously dismissed from both the agency and the band. He had been working in the office with Rik Gunnell, and, as the office became more and more successful, Mick and Rik had started fighting. The Blue Flames found themselves another tenor saxophone player in the form of Peter Coe, a man in his mid-thirties (the rest of the group were still barely in their twenties).

Eventually, they settled on a front line with Peter Coe on tenor and Glenn Hughes on baritone. Colin Green had rejoined the band on guitar and Speedy Acquaye was on conga drums, while Eddie "Tan Tan" Thornton, a Jamaican trumpet player who used to drop in occasionally from the society clubs, also joined as a permanent member. When Tex Makins came back into the band replacing Boots Slade on bass, the Blue Flames achieved their final line-up.

Georgie's relationship with Carmen continued to mature, and both Colin and Tex Makins had stable relationships, so the three couples all rented apartments together in the same block in Colney Hatch Lane, Muswell Hill, North London. "We were all living close together, in separate apartments as neighbours with our respective girlfriends. And that put another slant on our lives, because domesticity and close relationships with members of the opposite sex all came into play. It *really* became like an extended family for a while."

Georgie didn't have a car. Nobody in the band had a driver's licence, but they were getting around. They had road managers. They took cabs. They got a band bus to take them with the equipment if they didn't have an extra vehicle. Georgie was quite content with the new stability and even started to compose.

Everything was moving nicely. He had established himself with Harry South and was planning to go deeper into the world of big-band jazz. The Blue Flames were playing great, really firing, and it seemed that everything was finally on the rails.

The Blue Flames guested on all the early British television shows, including *Ready Steady Go!*, which was filmed at Rediffusion Studios in Wembley. It had an exciting live atmosphere with chaotic camera work: it was one of the first TV programmes that allowed teenagers on the studio floor, dancing at random, with the camera moving inside the crowd and across the stage. Most of the musicians on *Ready Steady Go!* used playback – essentially singing to a backing tape. But when the UK Musician's Union negotiated an agreement with the TV company requiring at least one band per show to perform live, Georgie Fame and the Blue Flames regularly got that gig. There weren't too many bands that could actually sound good live – particularly in a television studio – so they were featured every couple of weeks. It was terrific promotion and transmitted the charismatic image of the young singer nationwide.

All the rising stars did *Ready Steady Go!*. "I can remember first seeing Van Morrison on that show," Georgie says, "with Them, the Irish band that he started out with. I think Van said that they'd performed live on that show as well. I remember seeing a clip of the Rolling Stones performing on *Ready Steady Go!* where everybody insisted they were playing live, but on the clip I saw there was a piano playing in the track and Ian Stewart, who was the band's piano player, was not at the piano playing. He was actually on his hands and knees fixing Charlie Watts's drum kit.

"The other shows we did were chart shows like *Top of the Pops* and another very popular television show called *Thank Your Lucky Stars*. These shows were a bit more plastic, really. But *Ready Steady Go!* had this great sort of live feel to it. It felt more like you were playing in the club, a continuous live atmosphere for an hour every weekend. It was one of the most popular music shows of its generation and it would inadvertently play a rather significant part in my own future.

"I knew it was only a matter of time before we got a hit record."

4 Yeh, Yeh

"Ever since that time I've had no illusions about that stardom thing."

Georgie Fame and the Blue Flames were in and out of clubs, recording studios and television programmes on a daily basis in 1964 and built up a large national audience. They had a small first hit with a single from the *Flamingo* album, the Rufus Thomas song "Do the Dog," and a fan club as well.

Georgie was buying all the latest jazz records, especially those by Mose Allison, Ray Charles and Lambert, Hendricks & Ross – pretty much anything he could get his hands on. One day, he came across Jon Hendricks's recording of a live performance at the 1963 Newport Jazz Festival. Annie Ross had left the group – it was no longer Lambert, Hendricks & Ross, it was now Lambert, Hendricks & Bavan, with Yolande Bavan, the Sri Lankan singer – and on this recording was a composition by two musicians from Mongo Santamaria's Afro-Cuban band: baritone saxophone player Pat Patrick and pianist Rodgers Grant. Jon Hendricks had put lyrics to this song. It was called "Yeh, Yeh."

Georgie roughed out an arrangement. It had a "twist" kind of feel and an upbeat chorus. It immediately got a big reception in the clubs – bigger than anything else in their repertoire. When the time came to record another single, Ruby Bard, a mainstay of the Rik Gunnell management agency, suggested to Georgie, "Why don't you do that 'Yeh, Yeh' song?"

So they ran into the studio – they were actually on their way to a gig somewhere – and set up the gear as if at a gig and recorded two tracks: "Yeh, Yeh" for the A-side and a kind of jazz waltz composition called "Preach and Teach" for the flip. The latter was a kind of a throwaway, written by Johnny Burch, with lyrics about the Flamingo club. The single came out and they thought no more about it, and carried on gigging.

A hit record is something that no one can predict. Why one song takes off like a rocket while the best-laid plans often languish in the bins is beyond science. Georgie got a frantic call from the office: "It's sold 35,000 records in one day." By the end of 1964, "Yeh, Yeh" was in the top 10. In January 1965 it went to number 1, replacing the Beatles' "I Feel Fine". A jazz twist had made it to the top of the pops and Georgie Fame was now an international star.

The recording opened up all kinds of doors for Georgie, and it allowed Zoot Money to take over the permanent residency at the Flamingo; Georgie Fame and the Blue Flames were now playing major dates. They'd still go back and play the Flamingo now and then, because that was their spiritual home, but the gigs were growing – and with them so was Rik's office. All the bands he handled were working as many as ten gigs a week; just as the Flamingo was becoming less of an "in place" to go, overseas offers started coming in.

The first Georgie Fame and the Blue Flames gig outside England was in Sweden on 31 May 1965. The band flew from Heathrow to Stockholm's Arlanda Airport. SAS was operating small French-built Caravelle jets, which had two little engines on the back and held about 80 passengers. The Blue Flames were seated in the rear.

They had a number 1 hit record, they were still travelling in economy class, but they were happy just to be on an aircraft going anywhere. As the plane taxied to the terminal building, a single-storey affair, they looked out of the back window to see dozens of beautiful blonde young Swedish girls standing on the terminal building, waving and smiling, some even screaming.

They couldn't believe their luck. It took a minute to disembark and by the time they were on the tarmac all the girls had disappeared. It turned out that the actor Roger Moore had been in first class. Roger was a big star from the TV series *The Saint*, which was particularly popular in Sweden because he drove a Volvo sports car in the show. "Ever since that time," says Georgie, "I've had no illusions about the stardom thing."

The record company was waiting to greet them with three American estate cars. They all piled in and drove north. "Our first job was up in a little outdoor park in a place called Furuvik," says Georgie. "This was to be our first job outside England, about a three-and-a-half-hour drive from Stockholm. When we arrived, we saw the place was packed with young kids, some of them crawling around on all fours. In those days, young people in Sweden could get their hands on hard liquor, and they would drink a lot of it – a little too much and a little too soon. By the time the band came on to play, half of the punters were actually too drunk to know what was going on. That was our introduction to the international audience.

"But they all seemed to love the band. After the concert, we drove back to Stockholm to the Forrester Hotel, a very nice place not far from the record company's offices. The next day we were due to play our first gig in Stockholm, at Gröna Lund Park, the famous funfair with big open-air stages.

"I had to do interviews in the hotel that day before our gig and I will never forget the first two I did. The first one, I met a journalist called Hans Fridlund – Hasse Fridlund as we called him. He was the music journalist for one of the big newspapers, *Expressen*, and he spoke like an American. His English was excellent but, because he knew so many American jazz musicians, he spoke American English, really.

"He'd heard one of my recordings where I had sung the James Moody saxophone solo to 'I'm in the Mood for Love', the famous Eddie Jefferson lyrics that King Pleasure recorded and made the hit 'Moody's Mood for Love'. It was a stock part of the Blue Flames repertoire. While I was having this interview with Hans Fridlund he said, 'Have you ever heard of Arne Domnérus?' I said, 'No.' It turns out that Arne Domnérus was a legendary Swedish alto saxophone player, and it was *his* saxophone that Moody had played on this famous 1949 recording in Stockholm. For some reason, Moody had been on tour in Sweden and had to borrow a horn to play this legendary solo from 'I'm in the Mood for Love', and the rest is history." That story was a wonderful bit of inside knowledge for Georgie, a personal connection to a sort of holy grail in the deep jazz tradition.

"That morning, I also had an interview with a Swedish girl named Kris Gustafsson, and I absolutely fell in love with her during the interview. She was so beautiful and so soft-spoken, I was kind of stunned. I couldn't really answer the questions; I was just gazing at her eyes. I think that this has happened to many other guys; I'm not the only one who has fallen for the charms of these Swedish girls."

After the gig at Gröna Lund, which was right in the centre of Stockholm, the band went for a walk in the city and quickly discovered it had no nightlife at all. At two o'clock in the morning they were still looking for somewhere to go and having no luck. "It was becoming daylight, the sun was about to rise, and it was like a perfect setting to make a science fiction movie, because at dawn the city was deserted – not a soul on the street except for the Blue Flames and myself and the road crew looking for somewhere we could have some fun. We were used to England, where you could go places till six o'clock in the morning. But in Stockholm: nothing!" It was the first inkling that their music came from a small, boiling scene in London that probably didn't exist anywhere else – and it was about to change nightlife around the world.

Next day they flew to Gothenburg. There they were to play at Liseberg, another big city park with funfairs, restaurants and stages. In Gothenburg, Georgie's Hammond organ simply refused to fire up. There was no Hammond organ engineer within hundreds of miles so they did the whole gig without it. It was perhaps the first time, since he had done his turn as a child with the bones at holiday camp, and stood flat-footed in front of a crowd, with no keyboard to accompany himself or hide behind.

In Copenhagen, they played at the Tivoli Gardens. Before the gig, the record company took them out of town to an historic mansion where a huge table was laid out for 30 or 40 people with wine and champagne and an enormous buffet lunch. At the Tivoli, Georgie noticed that the Oscar Peterson Trio was playing in another venue at the park so when he finished his set he dashed over to catch one of his piano-playing heroes, feeling that a rising tide was lifting all ships, including his own.

Not long after this tour, in the summer of 1965, Georgie received a call from his manager informing him that the Tamla Motown Revue was coming over to England with the Supremes, Little Stevie Wonder, Smokey Robinson and the Miracles, the Temptations, and Martha and the Vandellas. They'd just done a big show in Paris and set up a British tour at the last moment: sort of "on the fly". The British music establishment – musicians, critics and promoters – were all in awe of this remarkable package. The Supremes had already had two number 1 hits with "Where Did Our Love Go" and "Baby Love". Nonetheless, for some reason, the package wasn't shifting tickets in Britain. They needed to add a British band to the package, compatible with the Tamla Motown sound. Because of the success of "Yeh, Yeh," the Blue Flames were selected. For Georgie, it was an unbelievable opportunity.

"We played two shows a night in big theatres all across England, where I'd been playing a few years earlier with the Larry Parnes touring packages. Yet, wherever we went, the houses were practically empty. We couldn't believe it. The music on the stage was absolutely fantastic. I've since read various articles about the history of Motown and the people at Motown referred to this particular tour as the 'Ghost Tour' because nobody came.

"But the music was absolutely amazing. We toured the country in a bus together and I'll never forget it. Smokey Robinson would be playing craps in the aisle of the bus as we were driving from town to town. And Stevie Wonder was constantly playing. He never stopped playing his harmonica – on the bus, in the hotel, on the street, backstage. We'd arrive at the next theatre for the evening's performance pretty early in the day, and while everything was getting set up and the Motown rhythm section, which was augmented by six or seven British musicians to give it a kind of big-band flavour, was sorting out the arrangements, Stevie would go straight to the piano and start to play – play, play, play.

"When the public was coming in, his minder Clarence Paul would say, 'Stevie you've got to leave the piano now because the public is coming in,' and Stevie would say, 'That's fine,' take his harmonica out of his pocket and continue to play walking up the stairs to his dressing room. He was just at it, all the time.

"One evening I was sitting in my dressing room and I heard this fantastic music coming from the room upstairs where the Supremes were. I walked up there and Florence Ballard was in the room. I said, 'Florence, what is that music?' She said it was a recording of Aretha Franklin singing 'Over the Rainbow'. It was the first time I'd heard Aretha's voice and it was unbelievable. I think it was her first CBS album. That was 1965 and I've never forgotten the sound of Aretha's wonderful voice spraying throughout the back area of the theatre."

Photo 10: Onstage with Stevie Wonder (aged about 14) and the Supremes.
Courtesy James Powell

The tour continued to play up and down the country. One night, when they were playing in Stockton-on-Tees in County Durham, the tour manager came backstage and said to Georgie, "You've been invited to stay at Wynyard Park. That's the home of the Marquis and Marchioness of Londonderry and they're here at the theatre and they'd like to meet you after the show." After the show, Alistair Londonderry, the Marquis, and his wife Nico came backstage and personally invited the Supremes, Berry Gordy and Georgie to stay at their huge estate just outside Stockton.

"We went to Wynyard House," says Georgie, "and none of us had ever seen such a place. It was a huge mansion on thousands of acres of parkland. We had our own rooms in this incredible private house with rolling lawns, a private lake and garden, the whole thing. We were all kind of in awe of it, including Berry and the Supremes."

Alistair was a proficient photographer and a keen musician – he played drums when he was at Eton and was a fan of Gene Krupa – with a wide knowledge of jazz. He adored Benny Goodman and in fact knew him personally. Alistair was part of England's new, young aristocracy.

The next day the tour hit Newcastle, only 30 miles up the road from Wynyard Park, and Georgie and the others returned to spend another night at the estate. In fact, they ended up staying there for a third night. During that last

Photos 11 and 12: With Diana Ross and Nico, on the fateful leg of the Motown UK tour when Georgie met Nico. The band were invited to stay at Wynyard Park, County Durham.

Courtesy James Powell

evening at Wynyard, Georgie went for a walk in the parkland with the Marchioness. And that's where "the thunderbolt struck": he and Nico – more formally Nicolette Elaine Katherine Vane-Tempest-Stewart – began their secret affair.

"Of course, I was still living with Carmen," says Georgie. "As we made more records, we didn't do so many late-night club gigs, so Carmen and I were very much a couple out to the clubs. Carmen would often go out with her friends a couple of hours before I would and we'd meet at the club. I rarely went out before midnight. She was friends with all the people who had little clothing shops in Chelsea that were becoming very trendy, like Granny Takes a Trip and Dandie Fashions, and she knew all of those young designers, like John Crittle, who were operating parallel to us, which eventually became the King's Road fashion scene.

"In the end, I didn't feel right about my affair with Nico, and I did treat Carmen badly when it came to the break-up. Not only did I cheat on her but I was a coward when it came to resolving the situation. She had every right to feel unjustly treated. But Nico pursued me like hell. She would turn up at gigs and she didn't brook anything. She had a healthy disrespect for authority, and she was determined to get what she wanted. I was in her sights, and I did my best to parry it and keep the balance with the band and all that. I told her, 'Look, this is my gig, this my life. These people are my family.' But Nico didn't care. She was just like a *blitzkrieg*. She didn't care what effect it had, even on her own children, on her husband. Whatever. She was just *there*."

Later on, Georgie learned that this whole affair was not as spontaneous as it first appeared and actually had its beginnings the previous year, in 1964, when he was on *Ready Steady Go!* Nico's sister-in-law had spotted him singing "Yeh, Yeh" and run to the telephone to call Nico. She said, "You have to turn on the television right this minute!" "And that's where it happened for Nico," says Georgie. "And of course that would have been before the Tamla Motown tour had even begun, so everything else that followed at Wynyard and beyond must have been firmly in her mind when I arrived at their estate."

He was only 22. Really still a kid. And he was now trying to keep private this clandestine relationship with a member of the British aristocracy. Naturally, he was quite paranoid about Nico's social status, as well as his own public persona: "I was out there gigging all the time. I'm on television all the time. I'm in the papers all the time. I have a fan club magazine. I'm everywhere all the time and suddenly I've got this clandestine relationship, which is really hot, but it's hot like a hot potato."

"I can remember the shiftiness of it all. One night, the band played up in Cheshire, not far from my hometown, maybe 20 miles away. Nico had come to the gig and the plan was for us to jump in the car and then drive up to the family estate. One of my oldest friends and his wife turned up at the gig and obviously they wanted to say hello afterwards, but I said, 'I'm sorry, I don't have time to talk now,' and I just jumped in the car and we disappeared. That's how intense it was getting: I didn't even have time to talk to one of my oldest friends, Alf Davis. So we just got in the car and tore off. She wasn't interested in meeting my schoolfriends anyway. She was only interested in what was going on with us. But I was still hanging on to all these other things."

Gradually, Georgie became uprooted from the life he had known. He felt exposed and shaken, as if he was being pursued by a heat-seeking missile. He had always had a great respect for authority, for elders and for the law in general, and this game of hide-and-seek didn't sit comfortably with his deepest self. But whereas Georgie had profound respect for the system, Nico had none, and she had the wherewithal to behave however she wanted: drive an Alfa Romeo, jump on a plane: whatever, whenever. He saw and felt his past becoming just that: past.

Many individual episodes combined to bring this home to him. For example, Rik Gunnell went skiing every year in Austria, and, after "Yeh, Yeh" was a huge hit, he said to Georgie, "Come on, I'm gonna take you skiing." They and a couple of club owners from outside London all flew to Zurich where they were going to take a short flight to the ski resort in Innsbruck. While they were in the transit lounge at Zurich Airport, there was a telephone call for Mr Clive Powell. It was Nico, calling from England, wanting to talk. He was only between flights for 40 minutes, but she knew exactly where and when to catch him. He was being pursued by a one-woman MI5.

Nico was extremely focused and Georgie was extremely flattered. She was a great beauty and, according to Georgie, "an amazing person". He was thinking, "I'm out of my depth here" and "Is this what I really want to get involved in?" But she was *so* determined that, ultimately, he fell. "We were both in love," he says. "But it took me a long time and a lot of adjustment to accept it for what it was."

"What it was" went like this. Georgie and the band were doing all the TV shows, making records that charted, and his popularity was increasing weekly, with more interviews, fan club magazines and mentions in gossip columns. Career-wise, everything was coming up roses. But, at the same time, he found himself in a serious relationship with a married woman, an aristocrat at that, while living a committed home life with Carmen. Nico increased her pursuit. She starting coming to Blue Flames gigs.

The band would be playing in a steamy club somewhere outside London and the road manager would come and announce, "She's outside in the car." He'd have to tell the band, "You go back to London in the car or whatever and I'll go back with Nico in her car." The relationship got stronger and it started to take its toll. This was obviously a very dangerous situation.

"At the time, I didn't know how much money I had because I never had my own accounts," says Georgie. "It was all dealt with by Rik Gunnell. But there seemed to be plenty of it around. Rik and I opened a club called the Bag O'

Photo 13: Old Compton Street, Soho, 1966.
Courtesy James Powell

Nails in Soho and it became a great venue. We gave Jimi Hendrix his first club date in London there. Paul and Linda McCartney first met at the Bag O' Nails while I was playing: they were at separate tables and while I was on stage singing 'Sitting in the Park' their eyes met and that was it."

Of course, Rik was using Georgie's money to finance the place, but Georgie was quite happy getting whatever he needed whenever he needed it and everything seemed to be fine. For several years, Rik had been encouraging him to compose: the Beatles had written all their own material, and managers and publishers everywhere were realizing that there was far more revenue in the composition than there was in the performance of music. But you can't just become a writer overnight. Unless you're a born with innate talent, like

Paul McCartney and John Lennon, it takes time and years of patience just to discover whether or not you have anything to say.

Georgie tried his hand at writing one or two things but it was slow-going. At first, he thought that every song needed to be personal; like the blues players used to say, "you can't write a blues unless you have the blues". Another misconception: he thought the blues had to be sad; the blues can be happy, joyful or spiritual – whatever you want them to be. The American folk singer Huddie Ledbetter (Lead Belly) once said, "The blues is a feeling and when it hits you, it's the real news." It takes a while to learn how to deliver the news in a song. Georgie was gradually finding his feet as a writer.

When asked which came first, the music or the words, the legendary American songwriter Ira Gershwin once said, "the phone call". Georgie discovered the truth in this joke one day when his manager called to say he received a message from an advertising agency representing National Benzole. This was an independent British petroleum company with stations up and down the country, and it was launching a promotional campaign aimed at the younger market. What they wanted was a piece of music that they could give away at their petrol stations: if you bought four gallons of petrol they gave you a floppy disc with this recording for free. They had no idea what the song should be about but they were paying a handsome fee and there would be royalties along the way. Someone mentioned the phrase "get away" – as in get in the car and get away – and that was the only clue Georgie had.

He had two weeks to come up with something. On the thirteenth day, he was sitting in the dressing room of a television studio outside Bristol with his band, waiting their turn to record something, when he suddenly realized that, at ten o'clock the next morning, the recording studio in Bond Street, London, was booked for him to record his original piece of music for National Benzole. And he hadn't written a thing.

There and then he picked up the guitar and started to strum. He got a kind of Bo Diddley rhythm feel going, and he cobbled together a vague idea in that brief time backstage. When the TV show was completed, they drove all the way back to London from Bristol and he stayed up all night playing the guitar and just singing whatever words felt like they fit the feel of the thing. At ten o'clock the next morning, he and the band regrouped at the studio.

The actual recording was done so quickly that guitar player Colin Green – who was actually the best musician in the band – didn't have time to learn it, so Georgie ended up playing guitar and overdubbing the organ solo. The producer was Denny Cordell, a man of impeccable taste. When they were listening to the playback – Georgie's manager Rik was in the hospitality room with the "suits" from the advertising agency drinking champagne – Denny said, "This is really good. This is very commercial. Maybe we could release this on a record. It doesn't mention anything about petrol or National Benzole."

They released it as a single for the general market at the same time National Benzole used it for their advertising campaign. By the time it got into the top

10 and the BBC were playing the hell out of it every day, the Corporation suddenly realized that they'd been playing what was, essentially, a commercial, and they'd been giving thousands of pounds' worth of free advertising to a petrol company. Eventually the song went to number 1 and everybody made a lot of money out of it. "In effect, this silly piece of music that took an overnight to put together and record had become my pension plan," says Georgie – "Getaway"!

After the success of "Getaway," his recording contract with EMI Records came up for renewal and Rik decided to strike a new deal with CBS. He negotiated a five-year contract, for which they paid an advance on royalties of £70,000, which was a huge amount of money in those days.

"I can remember the day we signed the contract," says Georgie. "We were in the office of Ken Glancy, the head of CBS Records in London. Right after the deal was done and we were having a glass of champagne to celebrate, Rik Gunnell sidled over to me and said, 'I want ten of that, right now.' Basically, he wanted his commission in advance. I don't know if it was because he had financial problems but he wanted £10,000 off the top, immediately, that day, in his bank account. Which I thought was a little odd."

It was to be a sign of things to come: what used to be about music and friendship was now going to be about money, plain and simple; what used to be about home and family was now going to be about royalty and royalties. Not just for Georgie but for the entire British music scene. It was blowing up and, in the midst of an expansion this large, with market forces taking over from emotional hunger, nothing could remain as it was. Once again, Georgie Fame was a stalking horse for many of the young British musicians who would come after him.

"That's how my relationship with CBS Records started, which wasn't a great time for me, artistically," Georgie says. "I had been nestled in my little rhythm and blues family for years – my band, my girl, my musical life – making music that I loved, and now that was obviously going to change. There was a lot of press about this huge advance they'd paid me and there would be pressure from all sides to make it back."

He and Denny went back into the studio to record things that they thought were still in keeping with the way he ought to proceed as an artist. Denny flew in some American musicians to London, great players like Chuck Rainey on bass and Hugh McCracken on guitar, to try to get some tracks down. Nothing really came out of those sessions. CBS became increasingly impatient; four or five months after signing the contract they still hadn't received the first hit single that everybody was eagerly looking forward to.

Coincidentally, the film *Bonnie and Clyde*, starring Warren Beatty and Faye Dunaway, had opened in the West End of London, and two very popular English songwriters, Mitch Murray and Peter Callander, had been invited to the premiere of the film in Leicester Square, black tie and all. They realized that the film was going to be a huge success and dashed home to write a song called "The Ballad of Bonnie and Clyde."

They sent the demonstration disc of the song to CBS. They saw it as a massive hit and sent it to Rik Gunnell with a note that said, "This is the song we want Georgie Fame to record next." When Georgie first heard it he thought it was one of the corniest things imaginable, certainly not the kind of material he wanted to record. But he knew times were changing, and there was that large advance hanging over his head.

The Beatles had just done *Sgt Pepper's Lonely Hearts Club Band* and even Zoot Money had thrown away his Hammond organ, packed up his Ray Charles LPs, started wearing hippie clothes and moved to California. Miles Davis, genius of jazz, started playing at the Fillmore, New York's premier rock 'n' roll venue. A lot of musicians from "the old school" were getting left behind in the wake of this mad rush towards a new era in the music industry; one had to do something to stay in the spotlight. But "The Ballad of Bonnie and Clyde" was a 180 degrees away from *Sgt Pepper*. It was corny.

At the insistence of both CBS and his manager, Georgie knocked off a quick musical arrangement of the song while doing a club date up in the north, near Newcastle, and sent the music down to London. In the middle of the following week, he flew down to London to record the song. It would be a decision that would affect the rest of his life, and his first clue as to the import of the moment was there when he arrived at the studio.

There were no musicians there. Mike Smith, the in-house producer at CBS, had made a backing track for him to put his voice over and there was nobody in the room but Mike and an engineer. Georgie had never made music in such a clinical setting. He went into the studio and sang, getting it down in one take, then went back to Heathrow and grabbed the next flight to Newcastle to continue working with his band in the club. His band had been hundreds of miles away when the recording took place.

A few days later he got a call saying that there was a problem with the recording: when they came to mix his voice with the backing track they discovered a noise they couldn't get rid of. He needed to come back to London and sing it again. But now they needed to get the drummer to re-record his part, this time over the new vocal. It was a Frankenstein approach, with musical elements being patched together to imitate a real moment – a technique that was becoming commonplace in the music business – which is why, if you listen to the record today, it sounds a little quirky and slightly out of time here and there. The finished version of "The Ballad of Bonnie and Clyde" had nothing in common with anything Georgie had done before apart from the charismatic sound of his voice. But that proved to be enough.

The record was released and instantly became a huge hit – number 1 in the UK and high in the charts around the world, including the US. To this day, Georgie Fame is the only artist that ever toppled the Beatles off the number

1 spot in the UK charts twice, first with "Yeh, Yeh" and next with "The Ballad of Bonnie and Clyde".

CBS was overjoyed because they'd started to recoup some of their huge advance. Rik was thrilled because he had his cash up front and more. And Georgie was consigned to go on a huge promotional tour around the world, miming the song on TV shows – always performing to playback – wearing a pin-striped suit, to fit the image of the gangster in the film, and carrying a toy machine gun while he sang, or pretended to sing.

It was exhausting and a bit humiliating. "I found myself going from pillar to post doing interviews with journalists, radio, you name it," he says, "the whistle-stop promo tour in America ... I just got into a complete daze by all this. You know, another studio tomorrow, another toy machine gun, another backdrop, maybe some dancers in the background, and I'm standing there miming to this corny song, when I'd spent all my career seated at the Hammond organ or the piano singing and playing rhythm and blues and jazz. I found myself standing up, pretty wooden, and wondering what to do with myself.

"I just had to keep thinking, 'Ah well, this is a big hit record and it's probably going to do a lot of good.' But, in fact, I don't think it did much good at all, even though it was a big hit. I still maintain it was a fairly corny song – a very clever song – but it wasn't the kind of song that I was happy recording. But I went along with the politics of the day, which meant, in the end, that my friend and record producer Denny Cordell was sidelined by my manager and CBS Records. And I was separated from my band.

"I found myself working with Mike Smith, trying to find material to record a quick album. They wanted a whole album of songs similar to 'The Ballad of Bonnie and Clyde'. I mean, what kind of task is that?"

He was learning, as Bob Dylan once said, "there's no success like failure and failure's no success at all"; when you get what you want, there's also a good chance you will lose what you had. He was learning to write the blues.

5 The Price of Fame

"That name took me everywhere my original name couldn't."

It would be an understatement to say his life entered a period of turmoil. He was starting a new family and the money was flowing in, for no good artistic reason. His emotional instincts were on high alert: the more he was being pressured commercially, the harder he worked to try to maintain an artistic foothold.

"Music was the one thing that had saved me when my mother died," he says, "and provided me a family when I first came to London. Music wasn't the problem. The music *business* and its impact on everything around me was the problem.

"Hit records are a double-edged sword. Back in 1965, when 'Yeh, Yeh' was a hit, I took the first money I earned and had a bathroom and toilet built inside the house in Leigh, because there never was one. But my dad was so taken by my success, when it was all obviously starting to happen, that he started referring me as 'young Georgie'. He quickly adopted the showbiz side of it, and I'm going, 'Dad, it's just a stage name.' But he went for it, big time. He would talk to his friends or even strangers, because strangers would get to him when they found out who he was. And he would sometimes put it about, when he'd go on vacations, 'My son...' I suppose he was living through me.

"And Nico always called me 'Fame', because obviously to her sophisticated, snobbish even, aristocrat heart, 'Clive' was just too common for words. It was a working-class Welsh name, and she didn't want to be associated with that. She had big plans for us.

"But Fame was all right with me. It reminded me of what the Black GIs used to call me, and so it was quite acceptable. Consequently, a lot of Nico's friends who became friends of mine, like Henry Pembroke and Simon Elliot, all these people that were in our social set, always called me Fame. So here I am, completely removed from the Black American GI scene, part of this British aristocratic social life, and they're still calling me 'Fame', which is funny when you think about it. That name took me everywhere my original name couldn't."

The name thing was particularly powerful in England, where promoters like Larry Parnes handed them out like tickets to ride and people from one class could suss out another person's social history just by their surname. "Clive Powell" was always a bit embarrassed by the name "Georgie Fame". Not the way Nico used it, because he felt it was always a term of endearment coming from her. "She used to call me that in all affection," says Georgie. "But it was obviously a conscious decision on her part that this would sound a lot better. And then her friends would hear her doing that and they would call me that, which was fine by me. I always said, 'Call me anything you like, you get the same person.' There's no point in making an effort to be something you're not. But it was an interesting process. A name given me for the purpose of showbusiness – to be an entertainer, not a musician – came to define me to a lot of my closest friends.

"Bill Wyman of the Stones had changed his name. His original name was Bill Perkins. He changed his surname to that of a guy who was in the Royal Air Force with him. It seemed to be the thing to do if you were moving in to the world of showbiz, which we were. We were moving into the world of showbiz, not the world of rock 'n' roll. It only became rock 'n' roll when the groups took control: the bands with three guitars and the drums. Because, up until then, we were all beholden to the impresarios and producers that wanted to put us on package tours singing three numbers with a house band. It was all singles. But then the group thing came on, particularly the Beatles, and blew the whole scene apart."

By mid-1965, when a lot of the British bands started going to the States – the Stones, the Beatles, The Who, the Animals, the Kinks and all the rest – they were all basically presenting three guitars and drums. That was what the Americans expected from the British "invasion". You could have a keyboard (like Manfred Mann) and even a Hammond organ (like Traffic) but basically the British bands were guitar-forward. And here comes Georgie Fame and the Blue Flames with two saxophones, a Jamaican trumpet player and an African conga player. No doubt, the William Morris Agency in America was thinking, "How can we sell this? We've got plenty of horn bands in the States. But where are the guitars?" Consequently, even while he had worldwide hits Georgie was having no luck with his band in the States.

"I never thought about putting together a band with three guitars and drums," he says. "It never crossed my mind to be in that kind of band. I never saw a place for myself in a band like that. Chris Blackwell at Island Records once accused me of being too eclectic and I didn't take it as a compliment at first, but later I did. Because, when you look at my first album, the one that we recorded live down at the Flamingo, we had two saxophones, a Hammond organ, electric bass, drums and percussion, and the material we were playing was the Quincy Jones arrangement of "Let the Good Times Roll" by Ray

Charles, "Baby Please Don't Go" by Mose Allison, "Shop Around" by Smokey Robinson and the Miracles, "Do the Dog" by Rufus Thomas, "Work Song" by Nat Adderley with the Oscar Brown Jr lyrics. And that's what the band was all about, really. And that *was* eclectic.

"So maybe it was simply that when you present that to an American agency or promoter he wonders, 'Where's the rock 'n' roll hook in this?'"

Some people said the Blue Flames' lack of popularity in the States was because they were an integrated band – they had an African conga player and a Jamaican trumpet player – but, more likely, the band was just too hip for the room. Hip musicians, like those who dug Mose Allison, knew about Georgie and the Blue Flames, but in the States the group remained "inside knowledge", much like the US blues musicians had been in England back in the early '60s.

Georgie also sussed out a deeper reason why he was not getting over in the States. "When 'Bonnie and Clyde' came along," Georgie says, "I was already band-less and wearing pin-striped suits and holding a toy machine gun miming to this corny record, pretending I was part of the movie. In a way, rock 'n' roll was seen as a complete break with the past and I was seen as *part* of the past.

"In America, the people who were playing in the eclectic, jazz and rhythm-and-blues tradition as we were, were being *driven out* by the British rock 'n' roll bands. Lots of the jazz clubs were closing or becoming discos or rock clubs. So I was stuck on the British Isles. I couldn't get arrested in the US.

"In the end, I don't know what the real reason was," says Georgie, "but it was very obvious we were not getting anywhere with this in the States. We didn't get a smell. And you can put it down to what you like."

In any case, when the British Invasion happened, Georgie Fame and the Blue Flames was not part of it.

One window that opened when the door to American rock celebrity closed was an opportunity to work with Count Basie. Of course, it placed him deeper in the jazz tradition, which only alienated more of his old R&B fans and gave the impression to the music press that he still belonged in the past. But it was a dream come true for Georgie.

He got the chance to sing with the Basie big band because of the *Sound Venture* album he had made several years before. At that time, he had little money but financed the project himself. "This was something I really wanted to do," says Georgie. "For me. I had managed to scrape the money together to get it started and I had to wait until 'Yeh, Yeh' was a hit until we had the money to go and finish it off, late in '65." The album was well received – it went into the pop charts and the top album charts – but it got the kids thinking, "What has he done? He's deserted us for the jazz scene."

And of course there was some truth to that. Because the day after he gave drummer Mitch Mitchell the sack, Mitch took the gig with Jimi Hendrix, while Georgie continued down the road that lead him to Count Basie and the jazz life. And while the commercial thing for somebody without three guitars was becoming pretty thin, the jazz side of things was starting to work out for Georgie.

Ironically, many years later, more than one rock 'n' roll singer, Rod Stewart being a case in point, in search of a second act turned to singing the "Great American Songbook" – jazz standards – and thus a route into maturity. But for Georgie it was a totally natural evolution in his musical education, and it came years earlier. He was musically wise beyond his years.

So in 1967, when Count Basie happened to be touring Europe and England with singer Tony Bennett, there were a handful of concerts at which the Basie band would be performing on their own, without Tony. Rik Gunnell had managed to swing it so that Georgie could do a concert with Basie in the period without Bennett. They booked the Royal Albert Hall in London and Georgie and Harry South flew to New York to meet with Basie and the musicians, talk over the programme and have a little rehearsal at a jazz club called Lennie's on the Turnpike.

Before the rehearsal, Basie's manager, Teddy Reig, came to George's hotel room in New York with staff arranger Chico O'Farrill. Georgie gave Chico a copy of "The Ballad of Bonnie and Clyde" and said, "Look, Chico, this has just been a big hit. It's the number 1 record in Europe at the moment and it's in the American charts. It's a real corny song but I just wonder if you could find a way of writing an arrangement for Basie's band and make it sound as if Basie was playing it for the first time?" Chico came up with a simple, swinging arrangement of the tune which sounded nothing like the original recording. It had that American swagger that played against the intellectualism Europeans were bringing to jazz at the time, and, of course, almost none of the stilted bravado of the original recording.

Georgie had turned to Harry South to be his musical director because it was the done thing at the time – guest singers usually brought along their own conductor – but there was a bit of back-and-forth between the two of them over the arrangements. Georgie wanted to maintain that loose, Basie swing, Chico's style, and Harry had written all these complicated arrangements for the *Sound Venture* album and wanted to go in that direction. Georgie was saying to Harry, "You know, maybe we shouldn't do those same charts because it sounds too much like British people, you know? Let's keep it as close to the Basie thing as possible: loose and swinging."

But Harry maintained a sort of cavalier London cockney attitude. "You know, if Ronnie Scott and Tubby Hayes can read it, the Basie band will be able to read and play it. The Basie band, they're all pretty good readers." "Which," says Georgie, "was completely missing the point. It didn't matter whether they could read it or not. It was whether the arrangements sounded right for the band. I didn't want to take the Basie out of the Basie band."

When they got into rehearsals at Lennie's on the Turnpike, the first thing that happened was Harry Edison, Basie's trumpet player, said, "You've got a whole lotta music here, Fame." "So," Georgie says, "I'm learning fast here."

By the time they did the night at the Royal Albert Hall, Georgie had sorted out the arrangements to his taste and actually walked on stage and said to the audience, "Welcome to my dream." He was thrilled to be there, but nervous too because of the flack he was getting from all sides: from the old jazz guard it was: "What's this young whippersnapper doing up there?" From the old Mod R&B fans it was: "He's deserted us and he's moved into the world of jazz." But there he was: smack dab in the middle again.

In the end, the gig with Basie was a success on all sides – the press liked it, the fans dug it, and most importantly, Georgie and the Basie organization got along well together. So well, in fact, that the following year Georgie was invited on a longer European tour with the Basie band. The tour opened in Frankfurt and, true to form, some of the German jazz fans left when he came onstage in protest of a young white English kid singing with Count Basie. After the show, saxophonist Eddie "Lockjaw" Davis, who was the straw boss of the band, called Georgie into Basie's dressing room.

"Jaws" said to Georgie, "Look the programme isn't working. We have to juggle it around and present it so it flows better." "It was a great learning lesson," Georgie says, "because I never realized that it wasn't just about walking out in front of the band and enjoying yourself, singing the song. You had to make it available to the public in the best possible way. It was just the sort of thing that I wanted to know about and had been thinking about, but Harry South had said, 'Oh, it's good enough for my band', without actually thinking, you know, you're playing with Basie. You're going into the Basie camp here.

"Tempo. Groove. Feel ... especially feel. And less is more. I just sat in the dressing room listening to everything that Jaws was saying because he was delegated to deliver the news to me – Basie was there but didn't say much, he just let Jaws do the talking. I picked it all up and we changed the routine a little bit and everything was swimming from there. Harry learned the lesson. He took out the tunes that I could see the band was struggling with.

"After that, everything was fine. I got on well with all the guys. It was a wonderful experience, a great help. And since that time, I've sung with all the best bands in the world and never had to worry about a thing because I learned it all from the master."

The Basie band was another musical family that had been together for years, going all the way back to Kansas City in the 1930s. They were loose, relaxed, serious about music but having a good time – just the way Georgie's own music always arrived. In particular, Georgie went to school on Richard Boone, a trombone player who got up every night and sang a blues by just making trombone sounds with his mouth. He used to bring the house down every time. Georgie remembers, "I was in the wings listening to this every night and thinking, 'Man, I wish I could do that.' And then one night I realized

Photo 14: With Jon Hendricks and Annie Ross ("Fame, Hendricks & Ross") at the Berlin Festival.
Courtesy Clive Powell

there was nothing to it!" That's when Georgie learned the art of scat singing, from a first-generation master – all part of the priceless education he was getting on the jazz road.

At the end of the tour, they did a final gig at the Berlin Festival in a tribute to the vocal group Lambert, Hendricks & Ross. For Georgie, this was literally his dream come true because Dave Lambert had passed away and Georgie was asked to step in for him, recreating the famous *Sing a Song of Basie* album – the same album that Georgie first heard so may miles ago in his friend Mike's basement flat. It was billed as "Fame, Hendricks & Ross", top of the mountain. Georgie told Jon Hendricks, "Look, I don't know it all but I've listened to it all and I've heard it all, and I took it all in." In the end, he managed quite a lot of it and it was great. "As far as I was concerned," Georgie says, "I was going from strength to strength."

He booked another night at London's Royal Festival Hall. The second half featured Georgie singing with Harry's big band, a kind of victory lap to celebrate the Basie experience. But the first half was Georgie and a new Blue Flames-type band, but with none of the original members. And the repertoire had changed as well. They did cooler material, like Percy Mayfield's song "River's Invitation," and none of the more raucous Flamingo stuff. This was still R&B but it was meant to herald a new direction for the Blue Flames.

CBS was recording the concert but it turned out there were technical problems with the tape. For a start, the general recording quality in the large hall was so bad that it was next to impossible to get control of the sound, and of course there had been little time in advance to overcome this. As a result, Georgie went into a studio the next week to record some tracks with a totally different line-up of musicians, again trying to make up the tracks for the "new direction" album. But, this time, he went even further afield into the jazz firmament.

He hired the finest jazz musicians he knew: saxophonist Peter King, drummer Tony Oxley, Gordon Beck, the pianist who played in Phil Woods's European Rhythm Machine, and a great jazz bass player, Jeff Clyne. "And," he says, "I did some of those Chet Baker things that my friend Mike O'Neill had written lyrics to, years before, including Chet's version of 'You, You're Driving Me Crazy.' It was about as far away from the pop scene as you could get. I thought it was my best shot."

It was clearly an artistic and an emotional pushback to the pressure he was getting from CBS to be more commercial, a thumb in the eye if you will. It was, he says, "a kind of a rebellious thing in a way. But I always thought of it, aesthetically really, as part of my musical education and my education in life. Travelling in good company, and being given the opportunity to improve and perform with your peers and your betters."

He didn't really have a plan. He was simply determined to follow the path he had started walking as a boy in Leigh, the youngster who saved his life with music. If it put him deeper into jazz territory, while it brought him further away from commercial stuff, that was fine with him. In the end, it only hastened the inevitable. The decisions that were being made for him by his manager and his record label, and the decisions he was making for himself, were growing further and further apart.

After the disastrous night at the Royal Festival Hall, and this radical new direction in the recording studio, CBS enforced their contractual rights and began choosing more songs for him to sing, ones that he would never have dreamt of singing himself. Yet, he says, he had no regrets. "When I would run into Mitch Mitchell, or any of the other musicians from my past, and they were now the biggest names in rock 'n' roll, I had no second thoughts. I thought I was doing fine. Where I was going musically was fine. I had a kind of financial security, although I never saw the money basically." But did he?

At the same time, all this chaos was going on with Nico. "It was tumultuous, really," Georgie says. But through the chaos and the unknown, he continued to follow the line of direction he had plotted with the music: "I don't think it was a rebellious thing. I don't think it was. I think it was just a quiet determination to persevere on my path. I'm thinking, look, Jon Hendricks has gotten me this far, from my jazz point of view. And my old friend Mike O'Neill has written these Chet Baker things, which I kept trying to introduce into my life in public. I even did one on a string album for CBS Records. They said, 'Do this string album for a change' when they couldn't think of anything else for me to do, and I thought, 'Great. Sing a few ballads with a nice lush string section. One of the obvious choices was 'Everything Happens to Me'. But they didn't want me to sing it with Chet Baker's trumpet solo, of course. That would have been my contribution."

There was another issue. After the enormous success of "Bonnie and Clyde", Rik Gunnell, who had the one of the most successful band agencies in London, decided to move up the corporate ladder and merged his business with Robert Stigwood. At that time Stigwood had begun to represent Cream, with Eric Clapton, Ginger Baker and Jack Bruce, and he also had the Bee Gees and a stable of film and theatre writers on his roster. So Georgie became part of the Robert Stigwood Organization. When, soon after, Rik was sent to the States to build up the company there, for the first time since he had walked into the Flamingo, Georgie was without a personal *consigliere*.

Meanwhile, Georgie was lumbered with this enormous advance from CBS Records, which he was trying to justify by coming up with material that he could stand behind and that would also pay back his debt to the company. One bright spot was the minor hit he had with the song "Sunny". It was a good song with a catchy hook written by an American R&B singer named Bobby Hebb, whose own version of it had topped the charts in the US.

The Blue Flames no longer existed – Rik had talked Georgie into breaking the band up and going solo, and CBS only wanted to treat him as a solo artist – so there were no overheads; you didn't have to worry about musicians on retainers. Georgie put the Hammond organ in storage and became a solo act, at the call of the enormous CBS organization, and was sent out on promo tours all over the world, particularly to the US, to do interviews, talk about his career and promote whatever the latest record might be, often miming to a pre-recorded track.

The experience was not without its virtues. In New York, Bobby Hebb himself picked him up at the Warwick Hotel and took him up to Harlem. First they went to Smalls Paradise and heard King Curtis. Then they went to Count Basie's bar, where they were quietly having a drink when a scuffle broke out towards the front of the room – there was a gun being waved around – so they hustled Georgie out through the back door. From there, they parked the limo at the back of the Apollo Theater, where Jackie Wilson was performing. When they walked around to the front entrance, the pavement was blocked by a large crowd, not to see Jackie but to listen to a sidewalk preacher. The guy standing on the soapbox was preaching Black Power. As Georgie was the only white face around, he felt like the preacher was pointing the finger directly at him.

It was an odd moment. Here he was, one of the foremost proponents of Black music in England, staying true to the course even as the business drifted west, and he had felt brotherhood with the Black GIs who had come to see him at the Flamingo – even to the point of blacking his face to feel that brotherhood on a deeper level – and yet standing there that day, he felt something for the first time: "naked in a fucking jungle surrounded by a bunch of tigers". This music was indeed a great teacher.

Spending time with Bobby, he gradually started to feel comfortable in New York. Before that he had been "a typical Brit: if you didn't know anybody in Manhattan, how do you know where to go, what to do? ... The first time I went there," he says, "I hardly left the hotel room. I remember Moondog, who used to stand outside the Warwick Hotel in his Viking hat with the horns on it, and that's about it. Yeah. I could go talk to him. But after a couple of trips with Bobby, I felt much more comfortable."

And then in LA, when he was staying at the Hyatt House Hotel on Sunset Boulevard – the bands all called it "the Riot House" because of the non-stop action in the hallways – coming out of the lift one day he bumped into Stevie Wonder. Stevie was standing all alone and Georgie thought, "I'll just go and say hello; maybe he remembers me." He went over and said, "Hey Stevie. You might not remember me..." and Stevie said, "Georgie Fame!" and they had a nice chat, standing in the lobby of a rock 'n' roll hotel in LA. "My career was in the doldrums and he was flying high but there we were. Three or four words and he remembered me." Georgie was again finding his family.

While he was in California, he received a phone call from CBS in London saying they were coming up with more ideas for hit singles. Now the choice of material was being made over a transatlantic telephone call. When he flew back from California he went straight to the CBS studios in London and recorded an album of songs that they thought were suitable. Once again, they weren't the kind of songs that he would have chosen for himself and they weren't the kind of material that really had a chance of breaking him out of the commercial trap he found himself in. Even songs like James Taylor's "Fire and Rain", while it is a good song, didn't fit right.

In a move to get back into a more permanent band situation, he and his friend Alan Price, the keyboard player from the Animals, decided to form a group together. Alan had left the Animals, and of course the Blue Flames were disbanded, so they used Colin Green, the original Blue Flames guitar player, and Clive Thacker on drums and became "Alan Price and Georgie Fame" (later to be known as "The Price of Fame").

Their original concept was that since they had so much in common – they both came from the same kind of working-class background and loved the same kind of rhythm and blues – that it would be easy to just go out and play some gigs together. They quickly discovered that most of the work that was available for them tended to be in cabaret clubs, particularly in the north of England. These were very successful clubs – but it was more like a working man's Las Vegas than a rich man's Flamingo. They really just wanted you to do your hit records; it was all just light entertainment, where everything was watered down to sell watered-down drinks.

The same aesthetic applied to all the TV programmes they guested on: all the well-known British prime-time shows like *The Two Ronnies* and *The Morecambe & Wise Show*. They became the "guest spot" darlings: musical guests who could fill three minutes with something light and airy – as long as you don't get too serious musically, you're beamed out all over the country on the biggest TV show of the day.

And yet, this too ultimately had a detrimental effect on the kind of work that they were able to get, because while they had intended to get exposure for the music they loved, they ended up doing all this middle-of-the-road stuff they hated. And even though it was high-quality TV work, the club jobs and concerts were getting further and further away from the original intention of their partnership. It's not that they didn't want to make money, but first they wanted to make music.

Then one night, when Georgie and Nico were having dinner at their favourite Indian restaurant in Fulham Road, talking about nothing really, Nico rather out of the blue announced that she was pregnant. Georgie's first thought was that, because after four years of trying she still hadn't hooked him, this was the endgame. "Perhaps that's a macho way of looking at it," he says, "but there you go.

"The upheaval was quite something I was carrying on a clandestine relationship with this titled lady, and every time I got back to my own place down in Chelsea, there was Carmen. The whole thing was on the verge of exploding and Nico was the fuse."

"I knew then things couldn't continue as they were and I couldn't continue cheating on Carmen and living this lie. At the time she was in Spain, where she used to visit quite often, and I just wrote to her and told her that I can't do this anymore. Didn't tell her why. Didn't tell her the whole thing. But that was it. I felt guilty for a long time afterward about the way I acted and the way I ended it."

On the 23rd of October 1969, Nico gave birth to a son, Tristan. She was still married to Alistair and she was still the Marchioness of Londonderry so Tristan was officially the son and heir of the Marquis of Londonderry. The idea of course was to keep the whole Georgie Fame connection hush-hush, but several months later, in early 1970, Georgie got the first inkling that it was no longer strictly confidential.

He was in Sicily, booked to play at the Palermo Jazz Festival on the same bill as Duke Ellington's orchestra. It was a great festival and a great honour to share the stage with Ellington, and Georgie was relaxing in his hotel room in the afternoon when one of the musicians came up and said that there was a journalist from the *Daily Express* downstairs asking for him. When the name "Londonderry" was mentioned he knew that the ruse was over. He managed to avoid the journalist, did the concert with the band and, instead of flying back to London the next day with the musicians, he booked himself on a commuter flight from Palermo to Catania and then on to Rome. From there he took another flight to London, all to avoid contact with the journalists.

This was to be end of his and Nico's long-term subterfuge. She had quite blatantly chosen to make the whole thing public. By the time he returned to London, it had become the talk of the town. Alistair himself wrote later in his diary that he had known something was up: it was "a not unsuspected relationship" which became confirmed, he said.

Why was Nico so driven to make the affair public? Georgie never figured that out. "I don't know," he says. "I suppose it's love. Or maybe it just comes down to the fact she saw me on television one night and thought, 'I'll pursue this.' At the time, the younger members of the aristocracy were mixing with the new kids on the block, and those of us who were making the music were suddenly the centre of a whole new scene. It was all going on in public. They were coming down to the Flamingo, hip young kids who were future earls were actually hanging out. In fact, one of Alistair and Nico's greatest friends, Robert Fraser, who was quite an authority on art, was at Keith Richards's house the night it got busted down on the south coast. Robert was in there, big time, in the inner circle. So I think that had something to do with what I was experiencing. The class structure was breaking down for sure."

The whole thing was a kind of perfect storm that took its time to break but, when it did, Georgie's landscape was totally transformed. When he and Nico finally married in 1971, he found himself thrown into a totally different world. It was quite a leap for him, this once relatively innocent young lad from the North. He was a believer in authority and everything that was good about the British tradition, started to have hit records and a band that was the talk of the town. It had all been going in the right direction, via the Flamingo residency, playing R&B and jazz and hanging out with the Black brothers from America, discovering this whole other culture that was welcoming and warm, like finding a family he never knew he had. And then suddenly he was pulled back into reality.

He had this huge advance – but so what? "What was I going to do with this money? Where's my band? And where's those Chicago soul ballads that we used to try to learn how to play and all that? They wanted to put me over as being a British version of Andy Williams or something like that, singing middle-of-the-road stuff, where the material was dictated to me by an in-house producer to justify the fact that they were paying us this huge advance."

On the surface, it might have seemed as if not much had changed. "When we all got together, the aristocrats and the musicians, the only difference among us was the accent, the way that one spoke, because everybody was excited about the same thing. Music appealed across the board. The tabloids had a field day with it because this wasn't supposed to happen, all these barriers breaking down, but it was just happening naturally. So I had to adjust to

Photo 15: Georgie and young Tristan on holiday in Wales.
Courtesy Clive Powell

this whole new lifestyle that I'd entered into with my wife, who came from a totally different part of society than I came from.

"The tabloids loved to publicize it when they saw an example of it happening. I mean they had it fairly right: 'Marchioness Marries Cotton Weaver!' in 20-point type. That was it. We were the extremes of society, coming together."

In the end, Nico didn't have any problem mixing with the musicians, and Georgie did his best to blend into her scene. She introduced him to lifelong friends – people she had known when she was married to Alistair. And Alistair always stayed close to the children. He never showed any animosity at all. Everybody got along fine.

But Nico had two daughters, Sophia and Cosima, from the first marriage, and Georgie was now their stepfather. He had been through something similar when his mother died so, without realizing it, when he saw certain signs he knew what they were. "From former behaviour patterns, I could actually relate to that after my mother's death. I tried to do the best possible job and I still have a good relationship with Nico's girls.

"Throughout the years, I have been determined to make a family work," he says. "When I was given the ultimatum, if you like, by Nico then, of course, I went wholeheartedly. And perhaps part of the reason is that I hadn't had the chance to do it when I was a child myself. I wasn't fulfilled. At first, the music, or the band, is your family. That's the surrogate family. But you still long for the blood family. What is so interesting is how the music plays a part in all this, getting you through it, motivating you one way or another, and keeping the family flame alive.

"When I decided to get married, I decided to set up out of town, away from all that madness, if you like, because this was going to be the new way. Everyone was buying a house in the country, preferably with a recording studio. It was the thing to do. First of all, I think it was Steve Winwood and those guys who moved out to Maidenhead or somewhere close so they could be in town in 30 minutes or so.

"But when I got married and was starting a family, when Tristan was only two years old and blood tests proved that Alistair Londonderry could not have been his father, when he was disinherited to officially become my son, I bought a house way out of the commuter belt, out in the sticks, so there wasn't going to be this commuting thing. I could get to gigs if I needed to, but people generally didn't commute from this distance. The kind of people we associated with had a house in town and a country pile to go to at weekends. Whereas we were going to live there all the time."

So, in 1971, with what was left of his advance from CBS Records, he said goodbye to all the nightlife that he'd been involved with since 1959 and bought a dilapidated old mansion in Somerset, beyond the commuter belt, outside a little market town called Wincanton. When he and Nico first went to view this house on a cold dismal February day, it was obvious the huge mansion hadn't been lived in, possibly for 30 years. It was rough, but Nico looked at it and thought, "This could be wonderful!" "She had a great imagination," Georgie says. But for him it called to mind a Hammer film set – a house of horrors.

They didn't actually move in until 1973 – 6th June, the anniversary of D-Day – because it of all the work it needed. By that time, their second son, James, had been born. At first, they all piled into the upper floor but, over a period of 18 months, they fought their way downstairs, renovating and repairing as they went. The place had 40 rooms and it took years to get the whole house done, including a huge orangery and a large dilapidated garden.

Obviously, a house of this pedigree needed a lot of money to maintain but the gigs were drying up. "I grasped the nettle, as it were," says Georgie. "I got whatever work was available, and I tried to stay true to my musical ideals.

"But I found myself in a situation where I had to ask myself, 'How am I going to keep this thing together financially?' I mean, we didn't live ostentatiously. It was a big house, but we didn't have the money that a lot of our friends and neighbours had – the bankers and aristocrats with family inheritances and all that ready-made money. We didn't have that. I was the breadwinner, and I was just doing it through gigs because the recording scene had gone pear-shaped. The recording industry had changed, and where do you go from here? So I worked where I could find work, as long as I could play the kind of music I was hoping to get away with. But there really wasn't a lot of it around.

"I found myself hanging out at Mike O'Neill's flat, when he wasn't working anywhere. He didn't have a band anymore. He didn't have a gig. He had a job as a cleaner, cleaning some Member of Parliament's house. Like doing the classic Eddie Jefferson thing: working in the kitchens. That's what Mike O'Neill was doing. There was no work for him in the business but I always took to him because he was so hip and so cool and so knowledgeable and never lost his enthusiasm for the music.

"Even when I was firmly entrenched with Nico I would go and hang out at his house. It was my escape to the other side, alone: the equivalent, I suppose, to a night of poker, out with the boys. I would go and hang out with Mike and stay late and sometimes sleep on his sofa and we would just talk about music and listen to Chet Baker. He turned me on to so many things, like Eddie Harris and things that he was interested in as a musician and as a lyric writer. And I was always looking to him for inspiration."

Georgie and Alan Price were still doing the occasional television appearance. They would be invited by the BBC to guest on all these popular comedy shows, but it would always wind up being a little musical insert between jokes, given two-and-a-half minutes to crank something out; and, of course, it had to be middle-of-the road and commercial. One day, they were invited to guest on one of Lulu's shows. Lulu is a well-loved entertainer and her 1970s programme had a big following. Alan said, "Let's do 'Back in the USSR' by the Beatles." So they devised an act where they sat at a grand piano dressed in tails and did an outrageous rock 'n' roll version with the full orchestra. They didn't know how to end it, so Georgie suggested that, when they got to the end, "The arranger could introduce the *Dr Zhivago* theme with strings and have it kind of descend into chaos." At that point, he and Alan staged a mock fight – they ended up rolling all over the floor in their black tuxedos with the camera moving off – and that was the end of their little cameo spot. Billy Cotton Jr, head of BBC2 at the time, saw it and said, "Who are those boys? Give them a series."

So they were finally given their own TV series. Here was the opportunity to showcase great music and musicians, they thought, to promote the best of the best: Georgie's idol Mose Allison, for example, or Randy Newman, a favourite of Alan's. But, in the end, neither Randy or Mose had a shot at guesting on *The Price of Fame*.

The programme turned out to be a Sisyphean effort. Georgie and Alan worked on it all day, every day, planning the songs and meeting with the arranger. After rehearsing all day Saturday, the programme was recorded in front of a live audience at 8 pm. "By that time," says Georgie, "it was 'Where am I?'"

They did have some great musical guests on occasion – like Delaney & Bonnie, the American duo that was touring England with Eric Clapton. But the guests could just hang out, far from the onrush of production decisions that Georgie and Alan were dealing with. They'd come in in the afternoon, sit in the dressing room for an hour, rehearse a bit, go and have a smoke or whatever, then come back and do their bit. Georgie and Alan were "like 16 tons and nose to the grindstone" all week. And, as they were working within the parameters of BBC2 TV's light entertainment policy, there was very little room for innovation or time for celebration.

In the end, this too went the way of previous middle-of-the-road TV shots the duo had done, and did very little to boost their individual careers. It even made it harder, in some ways. "Perhaps, because we were two people who looked similar, certainly played similarly and used two keyboards, to this day people think he's me and I'm him. It was ironic, but it certainly didn't help our plans to further our individual careers."

The gigs that did come in as a result of the TV show were more cabaret clubs up north, where people like Lulu were making fortunes. They'd pack them out. But they just wanted to hear your hits. Alan would do "House of the Rising Sun" and Georgie would do "Yeh, Yeh" and clearly the whole thing still wasn't going anywhere.

"We thought it would be a great opportunity to do something, and further ourselves musically and really have a ball doing the kind of things we liked to do," says Georgie. "But the system within which we were working didn't allow it. It also dictated the live work we could get as well. As the music ultimately became about the business – when the business took over the music – there was no longer room for the kinds of things we loved."

While Georgie had been dealing with *The Price of Fame*, the world around him – the business structure, the social structure, the economic structure – had been morphing into something he never expected. To him, pursuing jazz music had been perfectly logical: "I'd been following the music as best I could," he says, "letting the music take me where it would. And like I always say in interviews, when they ask me, 'Why did you move into jazz?' well it's a natural progression. Look, even John Coltrane used to walk the bar in Philadelphia, playing rock 'n' roll." But in the few short years between his first hit and his second hit – the two songs that knocked the Beatles off the number 1 spot – the musical world had turned; by the '70s, the music business was mostly all business.

Alan Price produced Georgie's next – and last – album for CBS, *Seventh Son*. Georgie called in some of the ex-Blue Flames and other top-level session musicians and they tried to go back to that musical stream in which he had so effortlessly swum before this whole four-year affair with CBS.

The title track, a Willie Dixon song, entered the charts, rose into the top 20 and for a moment there was a bit of a splash in the music press. He even did *Top of the Pops* again. And he thought, "This is great," because he had done it with this classic song that he had learned from a Mose Allison record. It somewhat renewed his faith and allowed him to leave the label on something of a creative note.

CBS got their four albums and their money back, plus more. But it was going to be a tough journey for people like Georgie.

Basically, he says, he "was pretty happy with the way things were going". He had an extraordinary house, a happy family and he was back to working in his own way, developing as a singer, pursuing the Chet Baker material he had always wanted to do and playing serious music gigs. A lot of his contemporaries – Eric Burdon and Zoot Money, for example – had moved to California to stay with the curve, if not ahead of it. Some dived head-first into the flower-power craze. Even Brian Auger went to the US because it was the place to be, even if you hadn't cracked it with the "Invasion". In London, things were getting a little thin on the ground.

By 1973, he found himself quite unencumbered. He was still involved with Rik Gunnell and the Robert Stigwood Organization, but the work was drying up. After flower power came groups like Pink Floyd and Led Zeppelin: stadium rock 'n' roll. The whole situation was moving away from Georgie's instincts and the good-time groove music he loved and deeper into the land of flashy guitars and huge amplifiers.

It would take a while for it to all shake out. In the meantime, there was his old friend Glyn Johns, who called him occasionally to play on albums he was producing. One was by the singer Joan Armatrading, another by his good friend Andy Fairweather Low. He also got a lot of TV commercial work, singing jingles and advertisements for companies like Maxwell House coffee and Woolworth's department stores. It paid well, it was over quickly, and it required very little of his musical soul.

In early 1974, there was an interesting opportunity to redeem himself artistically when Chris Blackwell offered to record Georgie for Island Records. Chris is one of the great figures in the music business, known for his taste and business acumen; like Georgie, he is a good friend of Glyn Johns.

Glyn came up with the idea to take Georgie to Tulsa, Oklahoma, and record at Leon Russell's church/studio, along with members of Joe Cocker's *Mad Dogs and Englishmen* band: Carl Radle on bass and Jamie Oldaker on drums. Georgie put together a bunch of new material, some of it in collaboration with a poet named Jeff Ryan.

They had written a great song called "Survival", a little dark but true to the times, and an out-and-out rocker called "That Ol' Rock 'n' Roll". The latter was inspired by his eldest stepdaughter, Sophia, who came home one weekend from boarding school and asked, "Georgie, have you ever heard of Jerry Lee Lewis?" It turns out all of her classmates had recently discovered the Louisiana rocker.

"We spent about ten days in Tulsa," says Georgie, "and we recorded what was quite a good album, I thought. It certainly had a good feel to it, and I was getting back into the pocket. There was one track, called 'Ozone', that I set to a real slow, Percy Mayfield, 'My Jug and I' kind of groove, and Bill Wyman thinks it's one of the best blues recordings he's ever heard in his life. So there was this good mixture, and I love that kind of Oklahoma shuffle that Jamie and Carl were producing. It wasn't the Flamingo pocket, however, which disappointed Chris Blackwell to a certain degree." Blackwell had been looking for the twist-and-shout groove of the past and the Oklahoma boys were going deep into the dusty plains of the American Southwest. It felt nothing like the past.

"Tulsa was a breath of fresh air for me because it felt pretty authentic," Georgie says. "When I got home, I said to Nico, 'I've had a fantastic time. I think it sounds great.' I really came back feeling good. But Chris Blackwell wasn't totally enamoured by the whole album, although he did agree that some of the tracks sounded really good. I mean, 'Survival' wasn't everybody's cup of tea because Jeff was a fairly bitter poet. But it was perfect for me at the time because it was my story: I *was* surviving."

In the end, Chris shelved the recordings and brought in Georgie's old producer Denny Cordell to try to change the direction of the project. Denny's idea was to go to Tennessee and work in JJ Cale's studio. Cale was a guitar player and singer with a cool, quirky style and a hero to many British musicians, including, Eric Clapton in particular. His studio was outside Nashville, and the day Denny and Georgie walked in it was Africa-hot. They saw this guy in shorts walking around pulling cables and putting in leads and it was JJ Cale himself. "I didn't recognize him at first, but when Denny walked in they were friends and we met," says Georgie. "It was like the story that Bill Wyman tells, when the Stones first went to Chess Records back in the '60s and there was Muddy Waters, changing the light bulb."

Denny called in a Brazilian bass trombone player from LA named Raul de Souza and flew *him* to Nashville to be part of these sessions. They also had Buddy Emmons, the world's foremost steel guitar player, and a drummer who, they were told, played on the original of Jerry Lee's "Whole Lotta Shakin' Going On". The first thing they recorded was a boogie-woogie, Louis-Jordan-cum-rock-'n'-roll version of the Ray Price song "Crazy Arms", almost bluebeat. Then they did a funny up-tempo version of "Getaway", featuring a ferocious Raul de Souza trombone solo. It was almost like a hillbilly samba.

Denny brought in a song written by Willie Nelson, "It's Not Supposed to Be That Way" ("...you're supposed to know I love you..."), which they did with a soft reggae feel and featuring JJ Cale. Overall, the sessions were unique. "Buddy Emmons was sliding away," says Georgie. "We had the reggae, the samba, the hillbilly, the Jerry Lee Lewis and the Louis Jordan boogie." It was all good but there was nothing holding it all together. There was no centre that told the listener who Georgie Fame was. If eclecticism had been his problem in the past, it was certainly not going away anytime soon in the future.

But Denny felt they still needed more tunes so they flew off to LA. Denny was born in Argentina and always dug Brazilian music, and around this time Brazilian musicians were moving *en masse* to California. Denny found four or five of these samba guys and they went into a little studio up in the hills that belonged to Mike Pinder the keyboard player of the Moody Blues. Georgie had been to Rio for the song festival and had written a samba or two, but this was a whole other order of clave. He couldn't really keep up with the Brazilian mob. But he did have two or three tunes – one written with Jon Hendricks called "Hot Stuff" – that were perfect for them. And Mike O'Neill had written an English lyric to a classic but not well-known Brazilian song called "San Marina". In the end, they came out with a few more good tracks. But, again, they were completely different from what had come before in Nashville and Tulsa, and none of it had anything to do with what Chris Blackwell had said he was looking for in the first place. The music was stylish but adrift.

One day, as he came out of Denny's house, Georgie ran into Jamie Oldaker and Carl Radle. They were recording with Eric Clapton at a studio just around the corner called Shangri La. It was owned by The Band; part of *The Last Waltz* was filmed there.

Denny and Georgie went up to the studio and discovered a weird, very stoned atmosphere with little musical activity. Eric was out in the back doing whatever he was doing. Richard Manuel of The Band was there, sort of floating around. There were all these rooms with different things going on but nothing was happening in the recording studio. Finally, Eric appeared and started to play something. There was no keyboard player, so he said to Georgie, "Do you want to play something?" Georgie played on one or two musical ideas.

Then Bob Dylan appeared. He was about to do something but just disappeared and never showed up again. He was reportedly last seen hitching a ride back to LA on the Pacific Coast highway. He just walked out back to the highway with his guitar and put his thumb out. "Strange days," says Georgie.

Meanwhile, Denny was spending a lot of time reading the *Greyhound Gazette*. "He bred greyhounds at his house in Ireland," says Georgie, "and he seemed more interested in the dogs than the music. And then the next thing I know, we're going to another studio in South Hollywood and there's Booker T., Duck Dunn, Steve Cropper, the whole Memphis crew. Denny knew everybody. So we got them to do a few tracks."

It was a rare privilege for Georgie to work with the musicians who inspired him to play organ in the first place – Booker T. & the M.G.'s! – but by now they've got the Memphis rhythm section involved and another horn section which included Blue Mitchell on trumpet and Raul on trombone. Suddenly there were four new tracks that somehow had to go with all the other stuff that had been recorded.

Photo 16: Performing on *The Geordie Scene* (Tyne Tees Television) on 16 January 1975, during the Island Records period.
Courtesy James Powell

"I think I was being pulled in so many different directions at the time," says Georgie, "because the music scene was doing the same thing: trying to relate with what had happened in the '60s, but at the same time being pulled towards what was happening in the '70s. This was '74, '75, just around the time that disco was breaking big in the States. And who did that? The Bee Gees. Of course, the irony was that my old manager, Rik Gunnell, was now representing the Bee Gees."

In the early 1970s, record companies didn't really know how to get what they wanted from these new young artists. Instead of foisting upon them corny songs from the past, they were basically paying people to get stoned, hoping that something would come of it. They were throwing money at groups in advances and saying, "Get yourself a house in the country with a studio and write your own material – that's very important because that's where the real money is – and come back with an album where we've got a piece of the publishing." The number of musicians getting stoned, playing snooker or taking a dip in the jacuzzi – doing everything at the studio *but* writing and recording – increased as the business itself grew from an industry measured in the millions to one that was valued in the billions. Soon enough, the artistic punters like Chris Blackwell who were heads of studios would be replaced by lawyers and accountants, and contracts would be rewritten so that all future monies came out of future royalties. Essentially, companies stopped putting up their own money; they loaned the money to the bands, and the bands owed them for everything. Everything became recoupable: ultimately, even a musician's life.

"I've never had a royalty statement from Island," says Georgie, "because the money that Chris put out for all this, he'll never get it back. But I always admired Chris. Even though he had a reputation in the business as a 'baby-faced killer', because he had a ruthless side to him, I really liked him. Like Denny Cordell, who was a great friend of his, he had great taste." There were still guys that loved music and were willing to put money into things that weren't commercial on the face of it. But of course a lot of that stuff never got released; in fact, almost none of it did. The numerous tracks Georgie cut on this particular adventure remain gathering dust on a shelf somewhere, and Georgie went back to working as he had been, still enjoying the ride. But work in the States, in particular, was impossible to come by.

In 1977, as Rik Gunnell was living the high life in New York, with a big office and a limo at his disposal, cruising on the energy of the Bee Gees' great success with *Saturday Night Fever*, Georgie tried to push him one more time. "I badgered him before our relationship finally broke up," says Georgie, "and said, 'Look, can't you get me a gig in America now that you're actually operating from here?

"Eventually, he got like five gigs, from New York to the West Coast. I took a quartet of great session players from England, and we started the tour in the Ballroom on the beach outside San Francisco. We went to Los Angeles and played at the Whiskey. And we played some funny place in Philadelphia with the Kinks on the bill. In the end, the whole exercise cost me £10,000." Of course, the ultimate irony, not lost on Georgie, was that Rik Gunnell would never have gone into the booking and management business if it hadn't been for meeting Georgie Fame and the Blue Flames down at the Flamingo.

While he was in San Francisco, Georgie went to see jazz pianist Thelonious Monk. At the time, Georgie's old friend Mike O'Neill had written words to Thelonious Monk's song "I Mean You". "It's a really funny lyric about a guy looking in the mirror," Georgie says, "saying, 'You're the one that brought me ruin, with all that evil doin'. You're the one I should be suin'. That's me there. I mean you.'" By then, they'd figured out you had to get the composer's permission, if not the publisher's, to actually go ahead and record it. So while he was in San Francisco and Monk was playing at the Black Hawk, Georgie thought, "Here is my moment."

"I just went there on my own," he says. "It was quite full and I got a little table for myself, just one chair, one little table, along the side of the wall. The bandstand is up ahead and Monk is playing, hat on and all that. And I'm half-way between the bar in the back and the band in front. It's noisy at the bar:

Photo 17: Nico and Georgie.
Courtesy Clive Powell

Jimmy Witherspoon's in there, having conversations with friends and they're all drinking and talking loud.

"I was trying to concentrate on listening to Monk. When he finished his set, he got up from the bandstand and walked through the club. It was not a very big club, and as he walked past me, I got up and followed him. When we got to the front door, I said, 'Excuse me Mr Monk, but you don't know me. I'm a musician from England and a friend of mine has written some lyrics to a composition that you wrote...' All this is going on and he's not looking and he's not stopping. He just keeps walking and I'm walking alongside of him saying, 'And we're wondering if you'd mind ... could we have your permission to record it maybe?' I got all that out as we got to the front door, and as he walked out the door, he turned to me and said, 'Sure, mothafucka, go ahead.'

"I immediately rang Mike and said, 'I spoke to Monk and he said it's okay.' Of course, we didn't know we had to go through all the bullshit with the publishers or whatever it was. Nothing ever happened but I did bite the bullet and I had the nerve to go ahead and ask him as he was walking out of the club. It was really fine."

In December of that year, when all the profits and losses were added up, Georgie Fame found he had a huge overdraft at the bank. Obviously, he was no longer playing on level ground. Where all the money went was never clear.

"In hindsight," he says, "I can see I really couldn't find my grounding because I was constantly trying to juggle things – which is why the recordings I did for Chris Blackwell were never that great and they didn't really make any impact. I had this huge house to maintain and I wasn't getting the income that was really needed to maintain this lifestyle."

One day Nico and Georgie were visited by Bertie Hope-Davies, the man who'd sold them the house in the first place. He said, "If you ever think of selling, I know someone who would buy this house from you immediately." Nico and Georgie talked about it. They'd been there for nine years and there was this large overdraft problem. So they sold the house for much more than they paid for it, cleared up the overdraft, and bought another small farm the other side of Wincanton, called Hook Farm, and set up home again.

"In the end," says Georgie, "I was glad to see the house go."

6 The Midnight Sun Never Sets

"...one of the most beautiful places you could ever visit on the planet"

Georgie was getting requests to work with all the great radio jazz orchestras in Europe – the WDR Big Band in Cologne, the NDR Bigband in Hamburg, the Danish Radio Big Band in Copenhagen, the Rias Big Band in Berlin – and he was doing a lot of work with the BBC Big Band, eventually making an album with them.

With Georgie becoming increasingly involved in the jazz world, it called to mind the joke that goes: A young boy says to his mother, "When I grow up, I want to be a rock 'n' roll musician." And his mother says, 'I'm sorry, son, you can't do both." Basically, while the rock 'n' roll world was moving on in its own direction, Georgie was continuing to grow as an artist.

On account of his continued dedication to jazz, he now had a library of big-band arrangements and orchestrations which were beginning to bear fruit. He would post the music off to a music director in, say, Denmark, Germany or Norway, jump on a plane, turn up at the rehearsal, do the concert, get paid quite well, and fly back home to his family in the UK.

One country where his work was particularly thriving was Sweden. A few years after his first visit – to promote "Yeh, Yeh," in 1965 – his office had received a call from a Swedish trumpeter named Lasse Samuelson inviting him to return, on his own, to sing and play with his band at the Golden Circle, Sweden's most famous jazz club. Georgie had a great time, met a whole new group of musicians, and began developing a following among Swedish jazz fans

His watershed tour of Sweden was in 1974, when Lasse invited him to perform on a TV show which broadcast live from Stockholm every Friday evening (very possibly a show called *Nygammalt* ["new/old"]). It was a great showcase for the Harry South and Count Basie arrangements and it became a regular invitation for him.

Sweden has a lot of big bands and Georgie worked with practically all of them over the years. Apart from Lasse's, there was the Tolvan Big Band in Skåne, near Malmö; the Sandviken Big Band not far from Gävle; the Norrbotten Big Band in Luleå; the Borhuslän Big Band just outside Gothenburg; and Fredrik Norén's High Coast Jazz Orchestra in Härnösand.

Most of these bands are partly composed of amateur musicians, but that in itself is a reason Georgie was drawn to them: the love of music at all levels of society and the Swedish education system that promotes it – there's a fine big band in practically every town. At a concert, you might see an old trombone player sitting next to a 14-year-old saxophonist; they're passing on the knowledge in way that doesn't happen in England. It was reassuring for Georgie to see big-band jazz as part of everyday life, not an occasional moment of nostalgia for a lost past.

Over the years, he played dozens of Swedish venues. In 1975 he played a concert in a prison situated 45 minutes outside Stockholm. Having arrived at the prison gates on a bus with the rest of the band, the gates opened, and they simply moved in, set up the equipment and played a swinging one-hour set. The real surprise was that the audience was mixed: the women, it seemed, had been bussed in to co-mingle with the prisoners for the concert, which was a half-dance, half-sit-down kind of club atmosphere. It seemed to Georgie that even in prison Sweden was more civilized than parts of England. At the end of the concert, Georgie was presented with a plaque from the prisoners' organization. "There was a code among the criminals in Stockholm at the time," he says. "In order to thank you for coming to the prison to play for them, they gave you this plaque, which was a caricature of a thief with swag over his shoulder and your name on it, along with the date of the performance. And if you put this plaque in the window of your apartment or your house in the Stockholm area, you would never have a problem with a local thief or burglar or criminal.

"Someone told me that, on one occasion, it did actually happen that a famous Swedish actress, who'd done a concert in this prison at Österåker, had put this thing in her window and some thief went into her apartment and stole things anyway. She contacted the prisoners in Österåker and said, 'Look this thing doesn't work. It's been in my window and somebody's come in and stole all my things.' One week later everything was returned to her, safe and sound. She got all her possessions back. So I've great faith in this plaque, which is still hanging on my kitchen wall. I had it in the window in my house in England for many years and it seemed to work there too – I was never robbed."

Another time, he did a tour with one of Sweden's most well-known rock 'n' roll acts, Beatmakers med Boris (Boris and the Beatmakers), which took him to the furthest reaches of the country. Following a hotel gig in Stockholm, they got into the bus at ten o'clock the next morning with all the equipment and drove … and drove … and kept on driving. They went through a place called Sveg and Georgie thought, "Wait a minute. Like, this has taken six or seven hours and where is the gig?" And Boris said, "No, don't worry we still have another four hours to go." Georgie had never spent ten hours in a bus before going from one gig to another. They finally ended up in the woods somewhere on the Norwegian border where there was a wooden structure which included a very small bandstand and a dance floor. "And where is the hotel, Boris?" Georgie asked. "Oh, there is no hotel here," he said. They had to jump in the bus after the gig and drive another hour before they found a little hotel where they were booked for the night. That was the second gig.

The final night of that tour, after zigzagging all over the territory, was in Umeå, many miles from Stockholm. His return flight to London was scheduled for nine o'clock the next morning from Stockholm, but the concert in Umeå wasn't going to finish until midnight: there was no way to get back in time to catch this plane. So, after the gig, he took a taxi from Umeå to Luleå, which is even further up north but had an airport. In the middle of the night, the taxi dropped him off at this deserted airport. There was frost on the ground and the building was closed. The taxi pulled away and Georgie was left, at three in the morning, alone and cold, to wait for his flight to Stockholm Arlanda Airport to pick up a London flight that left at 7 am. He rattled a few doors until he found one that was open and led into a small office. "There was nothing in it but a table and a desk," he says, "but it was inside and it was warm. Well it wasn't warm but it wasn't cold. So I sat in this place for three hours until they actually opened the airport and I could walk into the terminal, buy my ticket, get the flight to Stockholm and get back to London.

"I haven't done that type of tour since," he says. Normally, because of his relationship with Lasse Samuelson, the tours in Sweden went perfectly. "He'd give me the dates, I'd say 'Yeah', jump on a plane from London, arrive at Stockholm; Lasse had copies of all my big-band arrangements so he had already rehearsed the band for two weeks before and I'd just turn up, have a quick soundcheck, do a fantastic concert and usually have a very good dinner afterwards. As I said, if there's a big band in Sweden that's worth playing with, you can bet that Lasse Samuelson and I have played with them."

Another home-away-from-home for Georgie was Australia. It was one of the first places that provided an ongoing residency for him, and where he had solid relationships with fans and musicians alike. He worked there every year and developed a crack band which he called the Aussie Blue Flames.

The scene in Australia reminded Georgie of England in an earlier age. When he was first invited to go in 1970, he discovered Aussie working men's cabaret clubs in just about every city. Called RSLs (Returned & Services League) they favoured rugby league, like Georgie's local team back in Leigh.

They were huge social clubs, with a casino, poker machines and a large cabaret room. It was casual – you could wear shorts in the bar – until evening when they would bang the "Ode", the memorial bell for fallen servicemen, and there was a moment of silence. Then everybody disappeared and came back an hour later dressed for the evening's entertainment.

His first trip to Australia in 1970 was like a geography lesson: the Pan Am flight he took from London stopped everywhere: Frankfurt, Athens, Beirut, Tehran, Delhi, Bangkok, Hong Kong. When they flew over Vietnam, the pilot announced that he was going to take the altitude up, into the safety zone, just in case, because the Vietnam War was raging down below. It was Georgie's first personal experience with the war that was tearing up Vietnam and causing so much controversy in the States.

At Sydney, there was a press reception at the airport. Because of his rugby league background he knew the names of many of the great players – and this was his passport into the world of "G'day mate". He was immediately cool. But the next day, Georgie noticed his name was on the front page of two or three of the Sydney newspapers in a controversy about the length of his hair; it was only just touching his collar but the headlines read: "Will they let him in?" The RSLs had a policy of "no hair on the collar". Nobody mentioned it at the press conference; they saved the drama for the next day's papers. At his first gig that night, there was a man at the door with a pair of scissors. There were youngsters turning up to see the gig and they weren't getting in until they'd had their hair trimmed, too.

He stayed in Kings Cross, where he inadvertently found himself pitched into another angle of the American war experience: in the room next to him was a man who was evidently on R&R from Vietnam screaming down the telephone line, telling somebody that he didn't want to go back to the jungle.

On that trip he also met jazz promoter and all-round rake Barry Ward, who took him under his wing and introduced him to many of the musicians who would later form his Aussie Blue Flames. The following year, Barry got him a gig at the Basement, Sydney's legendary jazz club. "Talk about good gigs," says Georgie. "That was one of the best gigs ever, and always was. Every night was a fantastic gig and we'd turn the place into our own scene. Business was always good. I played there every year. Sometimes I would just go and play in the Basement for two or three weeks and maybe get the odd gig in Queensland.

"I had a wonderful relationship with Keith Stirling, the trumpet player, who was a senior member and a guru of the Aussie Blue Flames – a bit of a Buddhist and a real knowledgeable and funny cat. He was one of those that started to explain to me how jazz was based on triplets and all that. Instead of going home, he'd come to my hotel room and we'd sit up until dawn listening to cassettes of Thelonious Monk or whatever. He was another of my mentors and a great cat to have in the band. He actually renamed the band. The original band was just 'Georgie Fame' and then one day he said, 'We're the thrill seekers,' and then it became, 'Georgie Fame and the Thrill Seekers.' Later on, when Barry put the big band together, he called it Georgie Fame and the Big Thrill Seekers.

"Because we *were* out there, seeking thrills and doing it all together, we had the senior member who was right on the case if we needed to be put back on the straight and narrow. If there was any missing bits of information, like the history of Louis Armstrong, he'd tell you all about it. It was amazing. We were like blood brothers."

One year, on flying out to Sydney he discovered that some of the musicians had organized a game of cricket. "Want to be in it?" "Oh yeah. Great." The next day, they all turned up at Centennial Park. "It was casual: just a few musicians on our team and the brother of an English cricket captain, Dave Willis. We had a couple of beers. It was all pretty easy, but it was *hot*. It was plus 40° Celsius and it hadn't rained in Sydney for a month or more. The ground was really hard. I'm out on the third-man boundary, way out, and the bowler runs in, bowls, and the batsman cuts it and it's coming my way fast. I ran to cut it off, to save the four runs on the boundary. I dive to stop the ball from going over the boundary, which I did, retrieved it, and I kind of bounced off the turf. I picked up the ball and threw it back and screamed in agony. I walked off and they took me to Sydney Hospital. They X-rayed and the doctor said, 'Yeah, mate, you've broken your clavicle.' And we hadn't even done the rehearsal yet!

"When we turned up at the rehearsal, which had been called for later that same night, the musicians are all sitting there waiting for me to arrive and I turned up in a sling. And they all went, 'That's it. The gig's off. No gig.' They all had been looking forward to it. But I had asked the doctor in the hospital, 'Look, can I move this? Am I allowed any kind of movement? Can I do that with my wrist?' And he said, 'Yeah, you can move it. If you move it too much it will tell you. It'll hurt.' He gave me pain pills. And so we went and did the rehearsal. I had a B3 and I had the organ bench, which is a big piece of wood. I took my arm out of the sling and the thing was to maintain this position for four weeks or something so this all heals up. And I'm doing that: I'm sliding up and down the bench. If I need it to go up or down the octave, I'm moving my ass along the bench to get there. And I'm playing pretty much on one manual. I'm not stretching this thing really; and it all sounds fine.

"So we didn't tell anybody. And the next night, the band went on stage and I left the dressing room, I took the sling off and it was hot in there. We always took a towel with us anyway, so I walked onstage with the towel draped over my wrist looking like a waiter. I'm maintaining this safe position. I did the gig, and everybody's going, 'Yeah, fantastic.' The reviews were fantastic. The band sounded great. Nobody knew the difference.

"Three days later, and the place has been sold out for a week, and the word got out about what had happened and what I had done, and suddenly the guys were writing in the papers, 'I can only say that he's not a whingeing Pom: he's one of us, mate.' Didn't let a broken bone interfere with the act! That's the kind of thing that the Aussies like. A bit of rough and tumble. 'Fair dinkum, mate.' But I got all the accolades I needed from the Australian press just by dint of doing that. I was always cool in Australia after that."

By the end of the decade he was basically going to Australia and New Zealand every winter, taking his family and having an extended Christmas holiday. His children were old enough to travel; now, anytime he had a job that was paying enough money and kept him away for an amount of time, the whole family would join him. He managed to consolidate family life and the work that he was doing. As the new decade dawned, it appeared his determination to follow the jazz path was paying the kind of dividends that he had always dreamed of.

The proof was in the album he made in 1981 dedicated to Hoagy Carmichael. Hoagy, a musician, film actor and composer, ubiquitous in the '30s, '40s and '50s, was a hero to piano players who sang, or singers who played piano. His songs – the best known was "Stardust", but there were dozens more that set the bar for smart, sentimental, carefully crafted jazz songs – were considered the gold standard for composition; they were of high artistic merit and also commercially accessible to the average punter. Plus, on the big screen, in films like *To Have and Have Not* with Humphrey Bogart, Hoagy was one of the coolest cats around.

Harry South had a friend who was a great fan of Hoagy's named John Lamb, and it was at Lamb's suggestion that the two of them make the album. The only thing Georgie had really known about Hoagy going in was that he was the composer of "Georgia" and "Stardust". But he did remember that, years earlier, Ruby Bard, the agent that worked in Rik Gunnell's office – the one who had suggested he record "Yeh, Yeh" in the first place – always wanted Georgie to do a Hoagy Carmichael tune. At the time, he was too busy getting into Mose Allison and never took it seriously.

Now, when Harry called, Georgie had no recording projects on the horizon. He had done a couple of albums with Pye Records, but they didn't do anything and the record company folded completely. So, if they were going to do the Hoagy Carmichael project, it was going to have to be an independent production; they were going to have to pay for it themselves.

John Lamb put up some money. Harry had a friend from his TV days who put up some more. Harry didn't have the money to invest himself but he saw it as an opportunity to do something great with Georgie. And both he and Georgie were friends with Annie Ross, who was also currently in London and at liberty. The three of them met and talked one night and, in the end, decided they had to do it.

Georgie researched Hoagy's catalogue and rearranged a dozen songs to suit his taste. In order to put the music together he had to get inside each song and sort his own way through the structure and then find the right key and approach for him and Annie to do it together. For example, on "The Old Music Master", which Annie sang ("One night long ago, by the light of the moon..."), he opened with celeste backing and then took it into a Fats Domino feel – and got Dick Morris to play a fantastic saxophone solo on it. Annie did the "jump–jump–jump" thing from Count Basie's "One O'Clock Jump" which she had done with Lambert, Hendricks & Ross. So he succeeded in making references to Lambert, Hendricks & Ross, Fats Domino and Stanley Turrentine, all on one single arrangement. All the songs were given a new treatment.

In the end, Georgie had to borrow money to fund the project. It was quite a change from the CBS advances of yesteryear, but, as the great saxophonist Lester Young once advised a young musician, "Son, you have to save up to play jazz."

On this record, he did "Georgia" for the first time, a song that would become a centrepiece of his repertoire. Another interesting song, from the point of view of musical discoveries, was a thing called "Drip Drop", which Roy Berry, Hoagy's publisher, had uncovered. Roy had done the deal for "Yeh, Yeh" with Jon Hendricks back in 1965 so he knew Georgie. He came across this obscure title written in the early 1940s – he actually found a copy of it in the BBC Library – and it was a kind of old Dixieland knee-slapper thing, but Georgie turned it into a Louis Jordan shuffle with a very simple groove.

His idea for the song was he would sing the melody: "Listen to my baby balling, drip drop, drip drop / If she don't get whatever she wants, the tears roll down / One more hour of this shower, get out the boats or we'll all drown..." Then Annie would do the "drip drop, drip drop" thing, while all the while Georgie's playing the Louis Jordan boogie. Then the idea was to get Dick Morrissey or Peter King to do a honking tenor solo in the middle. But, when the time came, both Morrissey and King were out of the studio, around the corner in the pub. As they listened to the playback, Georgie said, "Let's just put the red light on and I'll go downstairs." He sang his own version as a scat solo, imagining what Dick might play.

When they heard it back, it sounded pretty good. "Now," says Georgie, "I always hated scat, but I sang what turned out to be the keeper solo on the whole thing so we didn't need the saxophone. But I wasn't about to let it go like that. It's got to have lyrics to it. Working under pressure, overnight, I put lyrics to my own solo. That was the most interesting track on the album from my point of view because that was a pivotal creative moment for me. It was the first bebop thing that I ever wrote." In fact, it was to be the first of many musical explorations Georgie would take into the land of "vocalese", wherein lyricists (like Jon Hendricks and Eddie Jefferson) would translate the musical improvisation of a jazz improvisor into the stuff of everyday narrative.

John Lamb had never met Hoagy Carmichael but he had been in touch with him during the production of the album. As an ardent fan and a persuasive sort of person, he asked Hoagy if he would consider contributing something to the project. Hoagy actually sent a tape, singing a bit of "Rocking

Chair" and playing a couple of phrases on his own piano in Palm Springs, California. Georgie used these two musical fragments to compose a ballad which he called "Hoagland", Hoagy's first name as he was christened. So two original pieces came out of that experience; for Georgie, the songwriting juices were starting to flow.

After they mixed the album, but before any decisions about how many copies to press and where to find the money to do so, Georgie was delegated by the other producers to go to Palm Springs and meet Hoagy. On his flight to Los Angeles he took along a friend of his, a filmmaker called Ian Winter; they rented a car and drove to Palm Springs.

The night before the anticipated meeting with Hoagy, the two stayed in a small, funky resort near Palm Springs called Two Bunch Palms. The next day they were to drive in and knock on Hoagy's door, hoping for a welcome but fearing a cold shoulder. John Lamb describes having written to Hoagy to say, "Well, they're going to come over and if you've got the time, maybe you could have a few words with them." Ian was determined to film whatever happened. So, that night found Georgie and Ian in Two Bunch Palms thinking, "How are we going to do this?"

"The next morning," says Georgie, "we drove in to Palm Springs. The car we rented was from Rent-A-Wreck because we didn't have any money; it was an old beater and it was wild. Hoagy lived in an elegant gated compound; we buzzed his number and his housekeeper answered. We said, 'It's Georgie Fame and Ian Winter from London, come to see Mr Carmichael.' 'Well, just a moment', and then the buzzer went. We drove in and knocked on his door and he let us in personally.

"I was aware that Hoagy Carmichael had probably never heard of me, coming from another generation, of course. But I was expected. It was a very hot day in Palm Springs, about 114°F, and he welcomed me, and the first thing he said was, 'Come in, boy. Keep that hot air out.'

"He was all sharp. Really sharp. We didn't know that he had just had 40 chemotherapy treatments. He hadn't told anybody. So he must have been feeling like shit. But he welcomed us into his front room and we sat and talked about music in general. Then he listened to the acetate and, afterward, he was very complimentary.

"He said, 'Well, I've had to rip apart so many versions of my songs, where people have messed around with them. But you've done a nice job.' And then he said to me, 'You have the makings to be a fine damn songwriter.' I thought, 'Yeah, I'm getting there.' It was worth the whole penniless project just to get that accolade from Hoagy Carmichael. It was the top of the mountain as far as I was concerned.

"Then he said, 'Back at the bar, there's a bottle of 12-year-old Ballantine's whisky. Bring that down.' 'Yes, Mr Carmichael.' I went and got the bottle down and we had a good drink. We stayed about three hours. He had a beat-up old

Photo 18: Hoagy Carmichael and Georgie in Palm Springs, California.
Courtesy Clive Powell

piano. It was one of those old writing-bureau-type pianos from the '20s: a classic.

"When he heard my version of 'Drip Drop,' he said, 'What? Did I write that?' He had forgotten it. But I knew the story of him chasing Bix Beiderbecke around for years and years: the verse of 'Stardust' is based on a Bix Beiderbecke piece that Hoagy had fallen in love with, but, after he composed it, he left it alone for a few years before writing the melody we all know as "Stardust". I said, 'Yeah, we found this obscure recording.' He was quite fascinated by it. I said, 'I just tried to take it more into my generation and give it bit of a boogie-woogie feel.' He was really tickled by the jazz vocal that I'd done, the scat solo with the lyrics and all that, added to his tune.

"As we were leaving, the last thing Hoagy said to me was, 'Just remember one thing, son. Doesn't matter what you sound like, my songs will make you sound great.' It was just a smart remark, like, 'Just keep your feet on the ground here, boy. Don't get carried away.' He had a twinkle in his eye and a wicked sense of humour.

"It was a great three hours."

Six months later, he received the news that Hoagy had died.

"I remember," says Georgie, "it was around Christmas time and Alistair, Nico's ex-husband, had purchased and renovated a beautiful villa in Tuscany where we all went for a vacation. Nico and me, Tristan and James, who were both quite small, all went to spend Christmas in Italy. It was great. And on Boxing Day we were invited to dinner at someone else's villa and took the kids along. There were probably about 20 people there, a big dinner but fairly casual. British casual. And, of course, at the end of dinner, we all go into the big sitting room and there's the piano. I used to get this feeling occasionally, when Nico and I got invited to certain dinners, that it was because I was going to have to do that bit after dinner, which used to piss me off a little bit. 'Please, would you mind?'

"Tristan and James walked over to the piano and said, 'Dad. Can we do a Hoagy Carmichael tune?' And I went, 'Hang on a minute.' I mean, they probably heard me working on the project at home, bits and pieces, and maybe they heard me playing songs from the album, listening through to the album which hadn't yet been released. But I had no idea that they were even halfway into it, or had any idea who Hoagy was. I said, 'Well, what do you want me to do?' They knew some of the titles, like we had done 'Up a Lazy River'. But they said, 'Do "Small Fry".' So they stood by the piano and we sang a little bit of 'Small Fry', one of Hoagy's most touching songs, about a young boy in the world. When it was done, I said, 'Look, it's past your bedtime. Let's get out of here.'

"We went back home and went to bed. And, the next morning, I was woken by the telephone; it was a gossip columnist from the *Daily Mail* back in London, Peter McKay. 'Can I speak to Mr Georgie Fame please?' 'Yeah, that's me.' And I thought, 'Here we go again.' Who even knows that we're in Italy? It was an ex-directory number in Tuscany; he must have called somebody in the family circle that told him, 'They're at Alistair's house in Tuscany.' I don't know how he got the number but he got the number. 'Yeah, okay. What is it?' Fearing the worst. And he said, 'Well, we just heard that Hoagy Carmichael died and we know that you went to visit him earlier and you produced this record. We were wondering if you had a quote. How was it to meet him?' So I told him, 'It was fantastic.' And that's all he wanted, just that.

"I put the phone down and I thought, 'Wait a minute.' With the time change, between Italy and California, I figured out it was pretty much the same time as he died that the boys came over to me at the piano and said, 'Dad, let's sing a Hoagy Carmichael tune.' I thought that was really cosmic. It scared me for a while. You never know, I mean, it could be just pure coincidence."

They released the album and put out a single in the UK which did nothing, so 5,000 copies went into the incinerator. However, the album was also released through a Swedish company and became very popular there, which led to more invitations for work in Sweden: with big bands, on TV shows and with small groups. Ultimately, there was even a television special produced in Scotland based on the album, with Georgie and Annie, where they had different sets for each of the different tunes. They pre-recorded the background tracks and did it *à la* Hollywood.

And so, as Georgie became associated with the music of Hoagy Carmichael, it was not just a personal honour but a sterling-silver jazz imprimatur that he carried. Hoagy had been spot-on: his music *did* make Georgie sound good. And, although it didn't sell many copies, the project created a bit of a stir – people were finally talking about his music again, as opposed to his family life.

"My wife and kids were still at home. The kids were still going to school and I'm still out there earning the money and I'm bringing it back. So, from my point of view, it started to matter less to me that there wasn't much happening in England."

Following the Hoagy Carmichael project, it was suggested that he do an album in Sweden called *In Goodman's Land*, a tribute to Benny Goodman. He flew into Stockholm and, along with expat American saxophonist Herb Geller, did two of Goodman's biggest hits, "Airmail Special" and "Flying Home". Next, Georgie sat outside on the terrace of the recording studio and wrote his first-ever attempts at lyrics to existing melodies. It was another breakthrough musical work for him.

"The next thing I know," he says, "I'm touring Sweden in a black tie with a singer named Sylvia Vrethammar, quite a big name in Sweden for singing one of the Eurovision songs a few years before. And I'm singing some of the Hoagy Carmichael material as well as the Benny Goodman stuff, and it's all blending in. And it's making an impact; I'm getting paid and I'm enjoying myself.

"That project triggered a contact from a good Norwegian piano player and arranger – and a great Tad Dameron fan – Per Husby. We had done some little gigs in Norway. Per knew my interest in Chet Baker and so he played me a recording of an album of Chet and George Coleman and there was a tune on there called "On a Misty Night" that Tad had written.

"Per had some money from a Norwegian company and he was going to make an album of Tad's things. He put a really interesting band together, like a Gil Evans kind of formulation, with Karin Krog, a Norwegian jazz singer. We sang a couple of duets together; we even did 'Lady Bird' and 'Good Bait' combined into one song; it was a medley. And he found a couple of other Tad Dameron things. One was called 'Accentuate the Bass', to which I put lyrics. Then 'Misty Night', of course; I was amazed that there weren't already lyrics to that because it was such a simple, singable melody. So I did lyrics to that as well. There was another great tune called 'That's the Way It Goes', which is a bit like 'Everything Happens to Me', and I wrote lyrics to the melody and then I wrote my own solo with my own lyrics to it.

"So now I'm doing gigs with Per and I'm singing the Tad Dameron melodies with my own lyrics. For me, it was another creative milestone, and something I wanted to do since I first heard Chet Baker and Eddie Jefferson and Jon Hendricks at Mike O'Neill's flat many years before." With the music of Hoagy Carmichael, Benny Goodman and Tad Dameron, Georgie was developing a serious profile as a jazz singer and raconteur. But there was one more jazz project he wanted to do: a tribute to Chet Baker with Chet himself.

"Back in Stockholm, at the Jazz Festival, I had been asked to introduce Eddie 'Lockjaw' Davis and Johnny Griffin who were playing together. The central point for accommodation in those days was the Castle Hotel in Riddargatan, just behind Nybroplan. Not a big hotel.

"I can't begin to count the number of wonderful times that I've had over the years in that hotel. This time, when I got back to the Castle Hotel, after introducing Jaws and Griffin, there was Chet Baker himself. So I approached him. I said, 'Look, I've got this friend in England and we started to listen to your recordings, and he put some good lyrics to some of your solos. And I followed his lead and now I've got like a whole bunch. I think there's enough for an album. How do you feel about doing an album together? It would be very easy to do.' My idea was to have him sing the original tune, whichever it happened to be. Or play it, if he wanted to, if he was up for playing it. Then I would sing his original solo with my lyrics or Mike O'Neill's lyrics, and then he can play his own solo or sing it out, whatever. Or we could both chirp the vocal. He said, 'Yeah.' Maybe he just thought there was a bit of money for a bit more dope in it. Who knows?"

But Chet was actually enthusiastic about the idea. This was in the summer of '87. The next year, the 13th of May, Friday the 13th, Chet fell – or was pushed – out of the window of the Hotel Prins Hendrik in Amsterdam, and he died, along with the dream project of Georgie and Mike O'Neill.

Throughout the 1980s, his contacts in Sweden and Norway kept him busy. He recorded with the great Norwegian jazz singer Karin Krog and from that received a number of invitations to work on Norwegian TV and do a tour with Per Husby's jazz trio around the west coast of Norway. "In September," he says, "it was one of the most beautiful places you could ever visit on the planet.

"So things started to look up again in the '80s, and I was happy working more outside England rather than trying to find work in England and putting a band together like the Blue Flames. The Scandinavian connection just kept opening up and, more importantly, I was singing a lot of jazz and I'd started to compose a little more as well.

"Then one day, while I was back in Australia on tour, my good friend Steve Gray (a great big-band composer and arranger) called to say he and I had received a special invitation from the Metropole Orkest, a wonderful orchestra in Holland, where we'd done several productions before – big band with strings. They'd invited us to come up with an original piece of music which they could produce. They gave us complete *carte blanche* – total freedom to think about what we wanted to do. It was January and the production was to begin in March!"

When he got back to England in the middle of February, Georgie found that Steve had already come up with most of the melodies. The musical, he had decided, was going to be based on the fictitious life (but based in fact) of a young, Black American girl singer who grows up in a small town in the US and goes to a gospel church and learns how to sing really well. She becomes a great success, but she's not happy with the multi-million-dollar sellers that she's recording for the company. She'd rather hang out in the clubs, sing the blues. It was actually a compact version of the life story of a dear friend of theirs – Madeline Bell.

So Madeline was the heroine of this musical, which they called *Singer*, and Georgie was "the narrator". It was 50 minutes long and the whole story was told in music and song. "It's one of the most profound things I've ever been involved with," says Georgie. "It's a wonderful work. Steve sent me a tape of his proposed melodies with rough working titles. I had two weeks to come up with all the lyrics for this thing, and at the time I'd not considered myself a particularly facile lyric writer.

"But, given this terrifying deadline and these wonderful melodies that Steve had presented to me, I got to work. I can remember waking up in the middle of the night in my bed thinking, '*Bang!* Something's happening.' And I'd go downstairs and put another tape on and listen to it and then do the lyric.

"I worked flat-out for two weeks and it brought me out of the closet as a lyricist; the lyrics that I did write in those two weeks were the best I'd written to date. I'm sure it was because of the pressure that we were under."

The finale of the musical was a very intense ballad piece – they were going to Holland to record this thing with the orchestra in two days – and Georgie hadn't written the lyric for it yet. At the recording session, while the orchestra and the conductor were waiting in the studio, he was sitting in a back room trying to come up with the right words for this final piece and it just wouldn't fit. It wasn't a very long piece but it had to be absolutely right because it was the last piece in the whole musical. He was struggling for about 30 minutes while they were all waiting and the clock was ticking. Finally, something clicked and he ran into the studio waving the piece of paper with the lyrics on it. They put the red light on and he sang it and that was the end of the musical.

"It was a wonderful experience," says Georgie, "and ever since that time, I've developed as a lyricist and I've been able to write my own songs with some ease." Again, Hoagy had been right.

"It was a lesson, really, in how to use one's imagination, because we always thought that songwriting had to be personal. But then, later on, you listen to people like the great Johnny Mercer – probably the finest lyricist of the 20th century – who once said, 'Look, you can write a song about this candle or this bedspread, if you use your imagination and create a situation, and it doesn't have to be personal.' As long as you can be lyrical and melodic, you can write a good song. It doesn't have to have happened to you." How often imagination trumps reality in the music business!

Over the years, Georgie's creative path was clearly more of an organic journey than a calculated career. The road often led him to unexpected, unplanned places, both physically and musically, and there were no shortages of harrowing moments and creative solutions. If one were to look back at the beginning, the one constant was a young man with his heart on his sleeve, trusting his instinct, shouldering whatever burdens were required.

One example, which had a bit of a comical aspect to it, occurred during the mid-1980s when Georgie was invited to play with singer Karin Krog and Per's small jazz orchestra at the Kongsberg Jazzfestival in Norway. And on the same date, unbeknown to him, his English agent had booked him with a very fine British jazz orchestra to play in a festival in the north of England.

It was a predicament, and he didn't know how to get out of it. But Per arranged it so that they could perform at the Kongsberg festival in the afternoon instead of the evening. So that day, Georgie jumped in his car at five o'clock in the morning in Somerset, drove to Heathrow, parked the car and took the 7:30 am SAS flight from London to Oslo. He arrived at Fornebu Airport in Oslo where the Kongsberg festival people met him and drove him to Kongsberg, one-and-a-half hours away. He arrived around midday, did a quick soundcheck and talked through the music with the musicians. The concert started at three in the afternoon. He sang his songs, then brought Karin Krog on stage to sing a couple of duets together. Then, while the band was still playing and Karin was doing some solo features, he graciously left the stage. Behind the stage, the festival had provided a helicopter, into the passenger seat of which he jumped and flew straight back to Fornebu. The helicopter landed directly outside the SAS flight for London, for which the steps were out and all the passengers on board. He climbed the steps, they closed the door and the plane flew back to London Heathrow where he had a commuter flight booked to take him to Grimsby in the north of England to play the other jazz festival.

The commuter flight was slightly delayed and he arrived at about nine in the evening. The English festival people met him at the airport, drove him to the venue where the big band had already been on the stage for 30 minutes, playing their own repertoire. Georgie waved to the conductor to say, "I'm here." They'd got his music and the programme all fixed, including one of the Chet Baker things and some of the Basie favourites. He ran on stage and sang for 30 minutes with another great jazz orchestra. Two in one day!

At 10:30 that evening – he'd been moving since five o'clock in the morning – rather than stay overnight in the hotel, the festival had arranged a taxi to take him wherever he wanted to go. When the taxi arrived he told the driver, "I'm going to Heathrow Airport in London" – a four-hour drive from Grimsby. The driver must have appreciated that fare.

Georgie said goodbye to all the musicians, jumped in the cab and told the driver, "I've had a very long day. I won't bore you with the details but I'm going to try and sleep on the back seat. When you get outside London and hit the M25 motorway, wake me up and I'll guide you round to Heathrow Airport to where my car is."

So he lay down on the back seat and was just about to go to sleep when the car came to a halt and the driver said, "I'm sorry, I've had a long day and I'm tired. My eyes are going and I need to rest for a while." Georgie said, "Okay, you jump in the back." The taxi driver jumped in the back of his own cab and Georgie drove all the way to London Heathrow Airport, woke the driver up and said, "You're at Heathrow; now you can drive yourself back to Grimsby."

Georgie jumped into his own car at Heathrow and drove himself home to Somerset. He arrived at seven in the morning, just as his wife was giving the children breakfast before sending them off to school, a little over 24 hours after he had begun the adventure.

"It reminds me what a long road it's been, really," Georgie says. "Just on the Chet Baker track alone, from Mike O'Neill's flat when we were kids singing along to Chet's records to running on stage at the last moment to sing one of his songs with an orchestra. It's all led to my becoming a writer and singer of my own material, which really was the dream at the beginning. But, along the way, you don't know why you make the choices you do."

7 Ulster Logic

"the start of a ten-year, intense relationship with Van Morrison"

"The first time I ever saw Van perform, he played a concert in Bournemouth, 30 miles from where we lived, and I said to Nico, "We've got to go and see his gig.' I'd met him briefly somewhere in a dark room in the '60s in London. He remembered it; I didn't. But I'd never seen his gig and he had a really good band.

That night, he didn't say jack shit to the audience. He played a little piano. He played a little saxophone. He turned his back on the audience and just got on with the gig. Never said anything; but he was roaring.

"In 1989 my son, Tristan, left school and secured a job at EMI Recording Studios. He'd always had a great interest in technology and very good ears, musically, so he took up a job at Abbey Road where he stayed for almost five years – as a trainee engineer at first, and then eventually he got to record quite a lot of influential artists.

"One night Tristan called me at home from his job in London. He'd had a call from Van Morrison's office. Not many people had my private home phone number but Van is the kind of person, I suppose, that wouldn't call me directly. So he got one of his people in his office to contact my son in London. Tristan said, 'Dad, Van Morrison's office called. He wants to talk to you,' and gave me a number to ring.

"I called him and it transpired that he was making an album and had a studio less than 30 minutes' drive from our house in Somerset; he asked me how I felt about playing a little Hammond organ on the album. I said, 'Sure, I'll jump in the car.' I drove the 30 minutes, went into the studio: there was a Hammond organ all set up with the headset. There were no other musicians around; it was a backing track. I put on the earphones and said, 'Okay, play it down and I'll get the feel of this thing.' It was just a straight-ahead 12-bar blues, I think in the key of E. As I was listening to the backing track I was sort of tootling along with it and trying to figure out what I would actually play when we did the real take. When it came to the end of the run-through, I called upstairs to the control room and said, 'Okay, put the red light on, we'll do it.' And Van came back and said, 'We just did it. That's it.' He'd taken the rehearsal and that's what went on the album.

That was the start of a ten-year, intense relationship with Van Morrison.

"After I played Hammond organ on just those couple of tracks on his recording *Avalon Sunset*, Van came over to my house and we started talking about the possibility of putting a band together, amalgamating some musicians that he knew in Ireland and some that he liked in my band.

"We're the same age. He comes from Northern Ireland and I came from just across the Irish Sea in Lancashire. I made a joke about the fact that we probably passed each other on the Isle of Man, this little holiday island in the Irish Sea where we used to go for our annual holiday and he would be going from Belfast. We probably passed each other in short pants on the promenade but we didn't know it at the time.

"Actually, that night at the dinner table, it was just me and Nico and our youngest son, James, who did the talking. Conversation from Van was quite light, but afterwards we went into another room to talk about what he wanted to do. We put two and two together and we bounced it around... 'How much do you pay your guys?' 'How much do *you* pay your guys?' All this kind of thing. He was quite interested in using my bass player and guitar player and one of my saxophone players, which is what we did. We just threw this melting pot together."

From the Irish side, they had Richie Buckley on saxophone and Dave Early played the drums. Neil Drinkwater played keyboards, Georgie played Hammond organ, and they used Georgie's bass player Brian Odgers and Steve Gregory, one of his saxophone players. Because Georgie had all the instruments set up in the barn at his home in Somerset, that's where they rehearsed the new band.

"It was the start of a really fruitful and enjoyable ten years for me," says Georgie. "I always found him an incredibly forceful presence on stage. He had really strong chops as a singer and he's a very intense performer. I think he's one of the great pop-rock poets, or whatever you want to call it. He's a great Irish poet; he just sets his poetry to music. The music tends to be more simple than the actual poetry. But he's a giant amongst performers."

Case in point: one of the first gigs Georgie remembers doing with Van after they got this new band together was at the Piazza in Milan, on an outdoor stage in front of perhaps 8,000 people. The band was sounding really good and Van was performing like hell and he was singing this song "When Will I Ever Learn to Live in God?" Georgie was playing along and listening to him and looking at the crowd, and suddenly he found tears in his eyes. "I mean," he says, "Van is one of the few artists who have actually, emotionally, reduced me to tears. Ray Charles did it to me once at the Hammersmith in London. But some of the performances I saw Van give when I worked with him were comparable to any performance by any great artist that you can care to mention.

"When I started working with him, he started talking to the people a bit more. I don't know; I like to think that we had a pretty good relationship, and we had a very productive time. A lot of people said that the band that we started off with, which was half of his guys from Ireland and half of my guys, was the best band that he had for quite a while.

"But there's no denying it: his reputation precedes him; he can be difficult. For example, he generally refuses to do any kind of interviews. I've always defended that because I understand where he's coming from, with that privacy thing and all. When I started working with him, it was right up my street, after what I'd been through with the divorce, and I was all for it. When he didn't do interviews he got the reputation of being difficult, but that reputation to me was pinned on him by the media. They couldn't understand why he wouldn't talk to them. 'What do you mean you don't want to talk to me? I'm the media. I'm the press. You must be crazy or difficult if you won't talk to me.' But I really admire him for that.

"At one stage we were playing festivals and I was being chased by some journalist from the *Daily Mail* that wanted to do a profile on me. I had heard about this particular journalist and I knew what he was all about, looking for gossip about me and Nico. I was refusing to even see this person who would suddenly turn up at the festivals in the middle of the country. I'd get a message from the third assistant roadie or something that this person is just outside, demanding an interview. And I'm going, 'There will be no interview.' This happened a few times. Then I realized that I was ending up in the same pocket as Van. But I was adamant about it and I didn't see any need for this because I'm on the road working with one of the greatest and most popular and creative artists and everything is fine. I don't need to talk about this driftwood or this other gossip shit. Naturally, they started saying that I'm beginning to be a difficult person or something, like they had already said that to Van. I thought, well, I'm happy to be associated with his camp on that score.

"I saw the way he thought. I *felt* the way he thought and worked, his *modus operandi* or whatever you want to call it. And I thought, 'Yeah, that's for me.' It's a bit like Mose. We talked about Mose a lot – who'd always stayed in the little clubs and never made a fuss. Never went out and said, "Hey, hey, it's me. Where's my interview?' or 'Where's my name on the front page?' or whatever. And we both agreed that that's the way to go. I mean he's in a far more comfortable position than I am, financially at least, but it doesn't matter. It's just the attitude and it doesn't prevent you from doing what you want to do musically. In a way, it frees you up to get on with it.

"Because," says Georgie, "when he performs on the stage, he bares his soul. Like Dylan, he writes poetry and puts it to music. He even said to me, 'How can I keep turning out these variations on six chords?' And I said, 'Well, you're writing the poetry. You have to put it down somewhere.' That's his limitation, musically, within how he works. But like all bandleaders, we like to surround ourselves with better musicians than ourselves and then let them blow and learn from them.

"So I saw him be difficult with people because he can get frustrated. When we used to fly to the States on long-haul flights, his manager used to book me with him in first class. He would say, "Go on and sit with him. He doesn't want to sit with me." But he might not have anything to say anyway. We both would just be reading books. Then maybe he'd come up with some questions and I think that was it. There was never any big long conversation, but I was always happy to do that because we have so much in common.

"Then, on the other hand, he'd keep you up all night talking about the history of one particular genre of the blues or rock 'n' roll: a bit like Bill Wyman that way. Even more than Bill Wyman. He could tell you who played on what record, when, everything. He was fantastic; still is. He's a great historian – a much greater historian than I'll ever be – and he cares about the music, for sure."

After about six years, Georgie left the band. The circus just got to be too much for him. It was putting demands on his jazz gigs and made his life unpredictable. "You couldn't reason with him sometimes. He was drinking; we all were. Now he hasn't had a drop for at least ten years – I did a TV show with him a few years ago, he was as straight as a die and he was performing great."

About six months after he left the band, Van called him and he agreed to go back. "I went in wholeheartedly and gave 150%," he says. "In total, I was there about ten years and he was very generous, financially, with me. I was already on my own feet with the work that was coming my way. But when I was working with Van as well, it was almost like back to the '60s when I was doing ten gigs a week. There was so much going on but I managed to balance it."

He went to America with Van several times – he had rarely been able to play there with his own band – and on one of those trips, when they were flying to New York to do the Beacon Theatre, they travelled together on the plane and "perhaps because he thought I was a bit closer to Mose Allison than he was," says Georgie, "He suggested that maybe Mose would like to be our guest on one of the concerts we were doing in New York. And so when we landed, I called Mose at his home on Long Island and said, 'I'm here with Van in Manhattan. Can we come over and see you?' So we jumped in the limo, drove out to Mose's house and talked together about music and the possibility of Mose coming up and doing a few numbers, which Mose gladly agreed to do. Also, John Lee Hooker was a guest at the Beacon. Van knew him quite intimately and he was one of Van's heroes. So it was a marvellous three days we did at the Beacon. It was a great day for us." It was also a great lesson in the blues, which, if you keep your wits about you on the road, you never have to stop learning.

John Lee had his own bass player so Van's bassist left the stage when John Lee came on. Georgie says, "I assumed he was his MD [musical director], who knows what's going on. Because we all know that those Delta boys, they just change the chord whenever they feel like it. There was no structure. Just 'let's change the chord now' and it all worked like that. So I knew there was that possibility, and I said to John Lee's bass player, 'Just give me a heads-up. We know he's going to change. We just don't know *when* he's going to change the chord. So can you just give me a quick hint a split second before it's moving so I know where I am and I can move with it?' And he said, 'Man, I don't know.' He was the regular bass player in John Lee's band, he had been working with him for years, but he didn't even know when John Lee was going to change."

This kind of root spontaneity is similar to the spirit that powers Van Morrison's best performances. "But whereas I'd like to think that perhaps John Lee did it from a biological, inherent point of view," says Georgie, "Van would often do it to keep you on your toes. What I call the 'Ulster Logic'. And he might say, 'Well, John Lee does it. We'll do it.' But he was doing it more from a stylistic point of view. Although Van is a great purist and he believed in that, absolutely. But I don't think he has written that many tunes with that kind of spontaneous movement in it."

Spontaneous movement was not just a state of mind; it was a fact of life on tour. In early 1990, Van and Georgie did a string of gigs for promoter Ron Delsener, including one in a large supper club in the middle of Manhattan. This night, there were to be several guests on stage. One was the great blues singer Jimmy Witherspoon. "Now I've known Jimmy for years," says Georgie, "since I first heard him at the Bull's Head in London with the Dick Morrissey Quartet, and he lived in England for many years. Jimmy, of course, is a legend. So 'Spoon' came out and sang a couple of tunes.

"We had all kinds of guests. We even had Richard Gere coming along to hang out backstage. And Richard Gere was a bit of a guitar player. So naturally somebody said, 'You wanna join the band?' And Richard Gere walks on stage with his guitar and joins us on 'Moondance'.

"Now at this point in the tour, Van liked to disappear about 45 minutes into the set. He'd go offstage. That was my cue and I'd do whatever I had to do to hold the fort until he was ready to come back. It would be just like 'Symphony Sid' or 'Green Onions'. It could be even more. It depended, but normally it would only be a few minutes.

"So, this time, Richard Gere has been up there and he's gone off, and Spoon was up and down, he'd done his little thing. Van's up there and then he disappears. Okay, guys, let's do this stuff. Five minutes later, there's no sign of Van. Where is he? Play another tune ... and still no sign of him. This goes on for about 15, 20 minutes. And the audience is starting to get a little bit restless ... but they're cool. They expect this kind of thing at a Van Morrison gig. In fact, a lot of his fans turn up *because* they don't know what to expect.

"So they all take it in their stride but you can feel a bit of a hustle and a rustle and a bit of tension is happening. Van eventually came back 25 minutes later. After the gig, I learned that Robert De Niro was in the joint and Van had gone back to his dressing room to talk to De Niro about some project and just left everybody roasting, including the public. Then he came back out onstage as if nothing had happened."

Delsener was known as a great promoter, in part because of his relationship with the musicians he loved. One night he took Van and Georgie and a couple of musicians to some little place at the bottom of Manhattan. There was nothing down there except dark little streets. They went into this building which turned out to be a little drinking club. It didn't look anything like a club, just a room with tables and chairs and a little bar in the corner which didn't even look like a bar.

Delsener suddenly decided to switch the conversation and poke the bear. "He said to me and Van," says Georgie, 'you guys don't know music. You don't know real music. You don't know shit. You don't know what real music is.' I said, 'What do you mean?' And he said, 'You don't know Louis Prima. You can't play real Louis Prima music, man. That's real music. You guys are just pissin' in the wind.' He was just winding people up. And I said, 'Well, yeah, actually we do. I grew up with Louis Prima. He was one of the stepping stones for me between rock 'n' roll and jazz, along with Ray Charles. Yeah, I know a lot of Louis Prima.' He's looking at Van and Van's not saying anything. He's probably trying to figure out: is he serious? Is he getting agitated or is he joking? And Delsener says, '$2,000 says you can't play Louis Prima's "Bona Sera".' And I said, 'I bet you we can.'

"The next day we went to the Beacon. I don't think we even rehearsed it or soundchecked it, we just decided on the key and we played 'Bona Sera' on the gig. We threw it in the programme at the end of the gig, as a kind of encore. Neil Drinkwater played the exact tango-piano bit on the front, the whole arrangement. We walked offstage and there was $2,000 in hundreds, in cash, on the little table by the side of the stage. We all shared the money.

"Van opened up a whole new world for me. In California, Junior Parker did several dates with us on harmonica. It was a wonderful experience; one night, Robbie Robertson joined us on stage in Los Angeles as well. Another day in LA, we had the day off and Van had been invited to perform on Herbie Hancock's TV show. Van's tour manager asked me to call Herbie and try to arrange the songs that we might do together. I called Herbie and said, "You don't know me but..." We arranged the tunes 'Moondance', 'How Long Has This Been Going On?' and a couple of others.

"When we drove to the studio where Herbie's TV show was taking place, there was Herbie, Chick Corea, Freddie Hubbard; we took our drummer, a couple of saxophone players and myself on the Hammond organ. It was a fantastic afternoon. It turned out it was actually Herbie Hancock's 50th birthday, so at the end of the recording we all went backstage and hung out where there was a huge birthday cake and several bottles of wine that we demolished. We all had a wonderful time. It was a day off but what a way to spend a day off. These things often happened when working with Van, especially in America.

"He was forever creating, always coming up with new ideas, new projects. Let's move in this direction, let's do this, let's do that. He wanted to do a jazzish album which I arranged, sorted out with other musicians that we knew, even recorded at Ronnie Scott's club in London to get the feel of a jazz club while we were recording. Again, our dear friend Annie Ross guested on one of the tracks. Another time, Mose was coming into London so we decided to do a Mose Allison tribute together with Mose himself, my friend Ben Sidran, who was Mose's producer, and Van, and we all collaborated on this album together.

"I think I must have played on about ten albums during the ten years that I was working with him and I never really had a dull moment.

"We had very good tour management. We were all keen. The band was really firing and was well organized and together. It was rare when things didn't work out as planned, but there was one extraordinary travel day I remember. We had a concert in Granada, Spain, in the '90s. I was driving to Gatwick Airport from my home in Somerset to meet everybody for the flight. There was a traffic accident on the motorway and there was no way I was going to get to Gatwick. I called Van's manager and said, "Look, I'm not going to make the flight. See what you can do and I'll get to the airport."

"When I arrived at Gatwick Airport, somebody was waiting to greet me. The British Airways flight with Van and the band had just departed. They arranged for me to get a seat on a charter holiday flight that was going to Malaga in about an hour's time. The plane was actually full but they arranged for me to sit on the jump seat on the flight deck, so I flew on the jump seat all the way down to Malaga. Van's manager collected me at Malaga Airport and we drove like hell to Granada. And, once again, we arrived about two minutes before the show was meant to start: the band was onstage, I ran up the steps, got on the Hammond organ, counted in the first number and off we went.

"And again, a few years later, we played a big open-air festival in England, in the Midlands somewhere near Birmingham, in a big park. Dylan was on it as well. Funnily enough, Geoff Dunn who was playing the drums, got stuck in traffic. So we delayed the start of our set, but he wasn't going to make it. I said to Van, "I'll play the drums." We went out at the start of the show and I played like the first two tunes on drums. And I was having a ball. Geoff finally arrives, runs out of his car and up onstage and I say, "No, no, no. Not yet!" I wanted to do more!

"Before that gig, Van said, 'Do you want to come along and say hello to Bob?' Like, basically, will you hold my hand? And I said, 'Yeah, yeah, I'd love to.' I had met Dylan very briefly somewhere in London in the early '60s. So we walk around to Bob's caravan. They were just these container sheds, really, nothing fancy, very sparse. Van and I walk in and it's, 'Hey, how you doin'?' 'Okay.' 'George Fame.' 'Yeah, yeah. I know...' There's some recognition, so cool.

"So then we're standing in this container dressing room and there's Dylan standing over there looking at a wall and Van is standing over here looking at another wall, and I'm standing here looking at the pair of them, gazing out over nowhere and there's nothing happening. Nobody's talking. So after a couple of minutes, I just said, 'Nice to see you. I'm going to go and take care of something.' And just left them to it, whatever it was. But there was no communication, which I thought was fantastic. These two poetic geniuses just standing there. They knew each other, of course, but there was nothing going on and I left.

"I had a lot of fun with Van. One of the funniest memories of my time working with Van was when we did the jazz album at Ronnie Scott's club. There was one song which Van didn't sing live in the club. It was a George Gershwin composition, 'How Long Has This Been Going On?' We had made a backing track of it and Van knew that I had recorded a version with my good friend and producer Ben Sidran, in New York City. I had listened to the Chet Baker version and put some lyrics to Chet's short trumpet solo and Kenny Drew's short piano solo and recorded that version on one of my Go Jazz albums. Van thought it would be a good idea to do another version where he sang the melody and I sang the jazz solo.

"Van turned up in the recording studio on the appointed day and there was nobody there except me and my son Tristan, who was the engineer. Van walked in at midday and he said to me, 'What's the name of that Norse explorer who went up to Newfoundland in 1100 and something?' I said, 'What?' I didn't know what he was talking about. And it transpired, because Van is a great musical historian, that in the original lyric by Ira Gershwin, there's a line that says, 'Now I know how Columbus felt, when he discovered a brand-new world.' The concept behind the line was that Christopher Columbus, in the three ships the *Pinta*, the *Niña* and the *Santa Maria*, went and discovered the USA in 1492. In fact, historically, I think they landed in the Caribbean but what the hell. They were over there.

"But Van had other ideas: he had heard of this Norwegian explorer that had gone to Newfoundland in 1100, way before Columbus, and he didn't want to sing this lyric about Christopher Columbus. He wanted to get it more historically correct. And he wouldn't sing the song; he refused to record it.

"So I had to pick up the telephone in the control room and ring friends in Norway. The first number I had was for Per Husby, the piano player. I called his number and his answering machine picked up. He wasn't home. Next, I called the telephone number of Ole Jacob Hansen, a great Norwegian bebop drummer, and his answering machine was on as well. Van is still standing there. He won't budge; he's not going to do it.

"The last number I had was for Karin Krog, the great Norwegian jazz singer. I rang Karin's number from the studio in London and she picked up her telephone. 'Karin. Hey, it's Georgie here. Listen, I'm in this studio with Van Morrison. He won't sing this song. What's the name of that Norwegian explorer they say went to Newfoundland in 1100 and something?' She says, 'Oh yeah, Leif Erikson?' I said, 'Oh bless you, Karin. Thanks.'

"I put the phone down and I turned around and said, 'Apparently, it's Leif Erikson.' He said, 'Okay. Put on the red light, I'll sing it.' And he sang about Leif Erikson on our version of "How Long Has This Been Going On?" I thought that was really funny and keen, one of the funniest moments of my life.

"One of the very few disappointments during my tenure with Van was the year Ray Charles came to him and they made a double header: Ray Charles with his big band and Van Morrison. We did the first half and Ray Charles did the second half, and I thought it's not going to get any better than this: I was working with Van; I've got Ray Charles for the second set and in the next dressing room – this is going to be like the peak of the career.

"But Van was restless at the time; something was going on in his personal life. I didn't ask what, but he had a private jet and he wanted to move every night. I don't know how many gigs we did – we must have done ten gigs around the country – and every night, after we finished our set, every night, I'd be dragged out with Van and a couple of his minders or friends to the local airport, into the jet and off to the next venue or back to Ireland. So I never got to hear Ray Charles. Except for one night, I think it was at Wembley in London, Van stayed. He didn't go anywhere. He did actually get up and sing a duet with Ray Charles. And that was it. I never got close to Ray Charles. I never actually got to shake his hand or anything because Van was in that restless mood and nothing was going to stop him from doing whatever he needed to do, not even Ray Charles.

"I used to talk to him: one of the big problems that he did have was he might do three or four gigs in a row, big gigs, and then not do anything for a month or so. In between time, he wouldn't think about singing. He'd be involved in other aspects of his life, like writing poetry or meeting people, talking, but he wouldn't do any singing. So he'd come back after several weeks off and we'd go somewhere to play and he'd be roaring on the first gig, blowing his brains out and we'd probably be sitting up very late in the night talking. The next day he'd go up and start hammering it again and there wasn't as much left. I can see it coming: on the third night, he practically lost his voice. So that's the kind of polarization you used to get with him – the extremities. There was no real middle of the road, no balance. It was all or nothing. He had no control over that kind of thinking.

"I remember one day he'd been to see Tom Jones perform somewhere in Wales or England, and he was quite impressed because the set was really tight. He said it was almost like segues from one song to another, and Van doesn't particularly like talking to the audience, doesn't feel it necessary to announce his tunes and all that, so he was impressed with how Tom Jones handled it, like *snap, snap*. It probably came from all of those years Tom Jones worked in Vegas. Whatever, Van was *really* impressed with that. He wanted us to be like that. 'Right, we're going to cut all this ... and it's all gonna go *bang, bang, bang, bang*.' I said, 'Well, sure, we can do that. All we have to do is tighten it up. But you still have to let us know what the next tune is', and then he'd come up against a brick wall.

"That's the way his mind works, bless him. And those kinds of episodes just show the human side of him. Underneath it all, he's as sweet as a nut. And you've got to credit him because, apart from the fact that his own work is great, he knows about everybody else's work. He's steeped in the Delta blues and he loves the *sound* of the music. He makes a lot of interesting sounds with his voice. The combination of the harmonica and his voice, sometimes you're wondering: is he actually singing in some language or are there just noises coming out? And because he has this broad, Northern Irish accent, which has never really left him, even though he spends a lot of time in the States and other places, when he's back in his own land, as it were, he can be as broad as anybody, and it's a very difficult accent to understand if you're not from that neighbourhood. It's closer to a really broad Glaswegian accent than it is to the Republic of Ireland and I think he uses that purposely sometimes. Perhaps when he's deeply into the emotional part of the performance, with his harmonica in particular, he'll occasionally revert to the Northern Irish accent, considering what it is up there with all the sectarianism and all that.

"I have always said – now I don't know whether it's true or not, I haven't spoken to anybody in depth about it – but I've always reckoned that they had their own logic up there. I called it the Ulster Logic, of which there is none. You talk about jive talking, really, or double talking, triple jive talking: something will be said to get a reaction out of you, but it's not the main thing; it's something back here where the real reaction that they want is. It's political, I suppose, because that whole scene in Northern Ireland is politics. It's like the religious sectarianism, but the hard Protestant stuff. I refused to play in Northern Ireland when I first got married because I married the former wife of the Marquis of Londonderry, and I thought I'd be an easy target, so I stayed clear of all that.

"So there was always that, but it never seemed to bother Van. To his credit, he's always had a fantastically across-the-board band: Black guys that used to play with James Brown, Catholics, it doesn't matter to him. That doesn't come into the equation. But Northern Ireland is a very interesting place to come from. Especially for someone like him who is so into John Lee Hooker and Solomon Burke.

"Onstage, I would hang on to every word because there's a lot of improvisation with him – I think that's why he liked me in the band because he could take off somewhere and I'd follow him; he could mention somebody or something in a song and I'd pick up on it and I'd quote whatever that person had done or something and that would excite him even more. Half the time, the band wouldn't even know what we were on about. But *we* knew and he dug all that. But there were times, even after all those years of working with him, when he put that harmonica in his mouth, or just the way he sang, you would think he was going off into some kind of scat or improvised jazz singing, for want of a better description, and the noises that would emanate: I mean, I didn't know what he was doing. Is he singing words here? What's he singing about? Is this just the Northern Irish accent that I don't understand or is it just noise? Is it just *sound* that he's lost in? Because he would get totally lost in the *sound* that he's creating. It was absolutely fascinating.

"You always had to be on your toes with him, every night, because you didn't know what was going to happen. He would always find a way of turning a song around: his own compositions, of course. He'd find another way of messing with it. And he'd do it on purpose just to keep you on your toes as well. That's part of the magic with the audience: they'd turn up because they never knew what it was.

"Amongst all of the conservations I've had with various musicians throughout my life, the ones with him have been among the most interesting, where we sat up all night talking about anything. It always started about music. 'How do you think so and so did this?' He was into Jon Hendricks and all of the jazz singers and Lenny Bruce, and he knows the history of it all, really. He knows all the writers, Kerouac, Burroughs; he's very well-read. And he'd talk about philosophy.

"I think he was basically a loner. Whether he was lonely or not, I don't know, because I know myself, living alone, I'm alone but I'm not lonely. I'm good with my own company. I'm cool with that. I'm not good in crowds any more. I think Van has always been like that. He's always been interested in, maybe not the occult, but religion has always been a crux for him to try to figure out. Which is probably why he dabbled in all aspects of religion. He's probably read all the books on every possible branch of religion, and he's probably come out the other end still an atheist. I don't know.

"When I finally left the band the last time, it was 1998. Van would always ring last-minute, when I was so busy doing other things, apart from working with him. This is one of the things that would frustrate me because my diary was pretty busy. There were a lot of things happening, and I said, 'Look man, just try and give me a bit of notice when you want to do something. I'd like to do it but I got myself in trouble a couple of times.' I had to cancel a gig with the Danish Radio Big Band because of him suddenly wanting to go to America for two weeks. I had to call and tell them, 'Sorry I can't do that because Van called me and I have to go do it.' And I never got an invitation to work with the Danish Radio Band again, probably because of that.

"This time, Van had decided he wanted to go to the States, so he asked me if I could go to America for ten days. There were four or five important nights at Madison Square Garden, in the theatre. The Stones were actually playing upstairs in the auditorium. Van Morrison and his band and Bob Dylan and his band were playing together in the big theatre. And I said to Van, 'I can only do three nights because I've booked myself to play at the Jazz Cafe in London – which was Vince Power's club. Vince was actually a friend of Van's, and he was going to be in New York when we were doing the gig at the Garden. Then the day after the Jazz Cafe I was booked to fly to Germany to do a production with the WDR Big Band, and the day after that to fly to Sweden to play the Jazz Festival with some Swedish musicians. I had these three dates in my diary and it was a good three dates, solid work. And that was it. I wasn't going to let them down. So I told him I couldn't do the whole run and he said, 'Well, come just for the three nights.' I said, 'Okay, that's very gracious of you.'

"After the third night, just before I had to split, me, Van and Vince Power were in the bar, and Van suddenly turns to Vince and says, 'You're stealing my organ player,' because I was playing in Vince's club the next day in London. I looked at Vince and said, 'Well, I'm going to be there, Vince.' There was no way we were going to change this. Then Van said to me, 'Can you get me somebody else?' He wasn't just talking about the next few nights; he was looking for me to come up with a permanent replacement.

"I said, 'You know, Zoot Money could really do your gig ... easily.' So we went around the back into a little room. I called Zoot from New York. 'Look, do you fancy ... we'll get you some tapes. You'll learn all the tunes.' He said yeah because it really got him out of a hole.

"Eventually, he learned all the tunes and went to Van's studio in the country in England with another three or four other guys that were already on the audition line. Van wasn't even listening to it. He was in his office on the phone. He popped his head in there and said, 'Argh, it's not happening.' And none of them got the gig.

"So that was how I left. There was no animosity. It was just a natural parting of the ways, obviously precipitated by the fact that I refused to cancel my gigs. I had been there practically ten years and, in the end, I have nothing but respect for the man. And I had a ball."

8 Cool Cat Blues

"I've had it with all of that jiving, no eyes no ears for what they're contriving"

"I first met Ben Sidran in Australia in 1988. Actually, Glyn Johns introduced me to his music in the early '70s, but we didn't meet until 15 years later when we played the Perth Jazz Festival on back-to-back nights. Two years after we met, he gave me the opportunity to record on his Go Jazz label. This opened up a lot of new doors for me and gave me the opportunity to sing songs that I wanted to sing, regardless of their origin, in great company and with fantastic

Photo 19: Georgie and Ben Sidran, Central Park, New York.
Courtesy Go Jazz Records

Photo 20: Georgie, Ben Sidran and Richard Tee in the studio.
Courtesy Go Jazz Records

musicians. A lot of people, I think quite rightly, have said that the Go Jazz albums we made were amongst my finest work and I would agree with them.

"I remember the first album we made together in 1991: I was on tour with Van in the States and I stopped in New York for a week to make the record that would be *Cool Cat Blues*. Ben had booked some great musicians for the date, including Robben Ford, Steve Gadd, Will Lee, Ralph MacDonald, Bob Malach and Richard Tee. Even Boz Scaggs and Jon Hendricks made brief appearances. It was a sign of Van Morrison's modesty and generosity that he also agreed to do a version of 'Moondance' with me on that record, no questions asked. And the version we cut with Jon Hendricks is a standout.

"I'd been working with Van for probably a couple of years and the whole time, which I was very happy about, I was classified as a sideman. I've always said I started my career as a sideman, playing piano for other singers, and I'm always happy in that pocket anyway. You don't have the responsibility of working out the set list and it's not your band. So I was very happy to be there to back him up to the hilt, whatever he wants. That's what I'm there for.

And if I get an accolade here and there, that's fine, but that just goes with the territory.

"With *Cool Cat Blues,* I had to come out of my sideman thing and go back into my own bandleader thing. This is going to be *my* album. Which tunes are going to sound right and good? And what's appropriate? I didn't mean it to be biographical at all, but it turned out to be really eclectic. I mean, I was really pleased that Ben liked the composition 'Cool Cat Blues' because it was written a long time ago with the poet Jeff Ryan, back when I thought I couldn't write lyrics. It was one of those things that Jeff and I came up with around the time we started working together, before I went to Tulsa with Glyn. So that tune had a lot of history.

"I wrote the song 'Cat's Eyes' driving home. I used to drive from London back up to Somerset quite a lot on the A303 which, at night, was an empty, easily drivable relaxing trip home. It's called 'Cat's Eyes' because you're looking at the cat's eyes on the road. 'I've been on the road, speeding on the straight and cuttin' the bends / I've played a lot of places, made a lot of friends' and all that. But, at the end, you go back home.

"That song, too, was a reflection on the trip to Tulsa, trying to get into that JJ Cale pocket. I was so taken with Jamie Oldaker's drumming and his versatility at the time that I wanted to document something or try to compose something that actually remembered his feel. I didn't want that feeling to disappear, even if I didn't go back to Oklahoma again. I guess writing that song was a way to keep the feeling alive.

Photo 21: Georgie and Ben Sidran in the studio recording *The Blues and Me* album for Go Jazz.
Courtesy Go Jazz Records

Photo 22: Stanley Turrentine, Phil Woods and Georgie.
Courtesy Go Jazz Records

Photo 23: Left to right: Ben Sidran, James Farber (engineer), Anthony Jackson, Chris Parker, Georgie, Will Lee, Hugh McCracken; Paul Shaffer (seated).
Courtesy Go Jazz Records

Photo 24: Georgie conducting the recording of *Poet in New York*.
Courtesy Go Jazz Records

Photo 25: Bob Malach, Georgie and Ben Sidran during the *Poet in New York* session.
Courtesy Go Jazz Records

"The lyrics to the saxophone choruses on the Louis Jordan thing 'Every Knock Is a Boost" were due to Ben prodding me, opening up a side of my brain to something that might have been dormant. When I listened to Louis Jordan's original version I thought, 'Geez, there's a lot of saxophone playing going on here', but it started to fall into place once I concentrated on it because Louis Jordan sang the melody in the first place so all I had to focus on was what they were saying with the horns. And you get the gist of the meaning of the song from what he's singing in the first place.

"So the lyrics to the horn solo fell into place and it was fun to do. It didn't take that long. It took longer to learn it, to sing it, than to write it. I walked into the studio with a piece of foolscap paper with the words: no notes, just lyrics. I had learned the melody to the solo on the road with Van Morrison after I had written the thing. I only finished it a week before the tour ended, but I had it down in my head so all I had to do was read the lyrics while I was there. It was a bit of a mouthful, but that again was somebody, in this case Ben, bringing out the creative juices:

"Every Knock Is a Boost": lyrics to saxophone solo:

I turn on my radio and TV check what people are sayin'
I hear 'em ranting and raving, all around the room
Maybe my ears are deceiving, I didn't go to college but I know what I believe in, man, what I hear is worrying
Rhetoric endlessly, chasing publicity, I might as well pack my bags, close the store, lock the door, and then throw away the key
Forever fussing and a-fighting instead of moving and a-grooving, everybody oughta lighten up before we go to ruin doesn't anybody wanna get along with anybody anymore I wanna know!
If we don't stop quarrelling, over-borrowing, causing sorrow then man, I'm afraid this old world of our is heading for a
Fall...
I don't care what people say, 'cause the whole world is in an uproar today
People are trying to oust each other, sister and brother
I'm gonna stay together today and let that other mess go its way
Everybody's stone crazy today
Every knock is a boost
I've had it with all of that jiving, no eyes no ears for what they're contriving
Pull the other one and you can listen to the bells are ringing on, don't wait for me 'cause in the morning I'll be gone, I'm outta here
I wanna give it to you straight because it's too late my friend, the party is over
Ain't no use raising your glass and drinking to the future
Because tomorrow's already here, and I'm seeing things pretty clear, the way the people are carrying on, it won't be long and we'll all be gone

So I gotta split the scene, catch you later, alligator, my plans laid, can you dig it?
Everybody! It's a boost, good news, buy booze, I'm so loose, you'll excuse me while I disappear
Sticks and stones can break my brittle bones but small talk never bothered me
It's kinda funny don't you know but when you really gotta go you gotta go, we're talking *ooblahdee, c'est la vie* just like they say in old Paree
When you see me coming! Raise your window. When you see me pass bye, don't you go cry
Everybody, every knock is a booooooooooooooooost

"Not long after we made that record, we went to Japan with the Go Jazz All Stars, and it was a fantastic feeling because going to Japan was like going to another planet, an alien culture. I knew a lot of successful jazz musicians and legendary players had been given a great chance to go to Japan and be treated with respect and paid good money for doing what they were known to do. Like Sonny Rollins, you know, Kenny Drew. They all went out there and were treated well. They loved it. So I knew that this was going to be a welcoming scene and it was very exciting. Being hailed as the 'Mod Father' was a bit of fun, actually.

"I'm very proud of the Go Jazz things, and the fact that ten years after we did *Cool Cat Blues* we did *Poet in New York*, a straight-ahead, stand-up-in-front-of-the-group singing thing, which was another dream that I had dabbled with at Ronnie Scott's. Of course, at Ronnie's I couldn't stop playing piano; on *Poet in New York* it was just like me being another member of the jazz quintet. It could have been two tenors, with me and Bob Malach. I think it was justified when the album won the Académie du Jazz award in France in 2001.

"Working with Go Jazz and working with Van during the '90s gave me the feeling that things were finally coming together and that all the years of work and travel were starting to make sense.

9 Hanging on for Dear Life

"Ever since the world ended, I don't get out as much."

Mose Allison

In June of 1993, not long after the first Go Jazz tour of Japan, Nico decided to throw Georgie a 50th birthday party. "We got a nice marquee tent and put it squarely on the lawn in between the house and the barn," says Georgie. "I called Mike Carr, the Hammond organ player, with Jim Mullen on guitar and Tony Crombie on drums, great little band. And I got some West Indian Jamaican catering firm in London to bring all the food down. I called a few people, family and friends. Alan Price came out with Zoot Money. People came from Sweden. Good music. All happening, great party. And Nico had never seemed happier. She was such a natural hostess, a fantastic hostess, that it was a great day, for everybody. And then everybody departed.

"Nico was hiding something. The next day, she showed signs of depression. I couldn't figure out what was wrong. Then she started to talk to me in kind of odd terms. I remember she was saying things like, 'You'll be okay without me, won't you? Because you've got your music.' I thought, 'Wait a minute. Something is really strange here.' And a couple of weeks later, she went off in the morning, in the car, and didn't come back.

"About a year before, she did have a failed attempted suicide. And she used to say to me, 'Look, what would you do if I wasn't around anymore?' And, 'You'll always have your music.' And I said, 'Well, that's only one part of it. What about the boys? We've got this family and everything is cool. We don't owe anybody any money. We've come through.' Everybody seemed to be happy, but there was definitely something missing in her life.

"The first time she tried to kill herself, she disappeared and I got very suspicious. I called the local police and they came from another town. It was one of the most demoralizing hours of my life. These three robots came into my kitchen and I'm telling them what's happening, the detectives. I said, 'Look, my sneaking feeling is that she's actually not far away in the neighbourhood. And she was driving, and here's the description of the car' and all that.

"But all they were interested in was making up a log of procedures. They were asking for telephone numbers of her acquaintances in London. And I said, 'Look, I've spoken to them. She's not there. She's around here somewhere.' After about an hour of getting nowhere with these policemen – they weren't interested in actually sending a search out for her or getting something out – I said, 'I'm sorry I'm going to do something about this myself.' I went and rented a helicopter at a local airfield and we did a tour around the forest area nearby. We actually didn't see it, but the car *was* there. And some foresters found the car and she was in it. She was alive. She had survived.

"I went up to the hospital and sat by the bed for several hours until she came around. When she came to, she kind of burst into tears. Instead of taking her home, I got her out of the hospital as quickly as possible and booked into a nice, quiet, comfortable hotel outside of Bath for a couple of days. We spent the time there until we both thought she was well enough to go home. Of course, I had been hoping that was the end of it. She seemed to be okay. Generally speaking, as it were. And this was all kind of confidential. There were only one or two people who knew about it.

"Annabel, her sister-in-law, knew about it. I told Annabel what had happened and Annabel said, 'Oh, she was always saying things like that when she was 20 years old, she was always banging on...' No help whatsoever. I said, 'Look, this actually happened.' 'Oh, but don't worry...' They didn't grasp the seriousness of the situation at all. But, from that time on, I was on my guard.

"The first attempt was about a year before she actually succeeded. We'd have conversations at home and I thought I was getting her back on the right track, really, because I was saying, 'The boys ... what are you going to with the boys? Are you going to leave me with the boys? Why do you want to quit?' She had done it once so the danger was that she was going to try it again.

"When she finally did, it was two months after this great party. Everybody had had a great time. She was a perfect hostess, and I thought, we're cool here. Then, on Friday the 13th of August, Nico went off. She said she was going to go shopping or whatever. It was late morning and normally she would come back just after lunchtime. She didn't come back, and around five o'clock a police car arrived and I knew immediately what had happened. It was like the same thing that happened with my father, when he came from the hospital after my mother had passed away. He got off the bike and looked at me and I knew.

"I said, 'Okay, where did it happen?' And they told me. They said that she had jumped off of the Clifton Suspension Bridge outside of Bristol. And my life fell apart, really.

"Of course, the press got hold of this. I had to go and identify the body in Bristol at the morgue. Later on there was an inquest, which was a fairly straightforward affair, but we couldn't keep this away from the press, obviously.

"Within 24 hours, there was a fleet of cars parked in the lane outside of my house. Luckily, we had big high wooden gates and a fairly secure thick hedge. There was a television crew parked outside, waiting for any glimpse of me or any members of my family. It was a bit of a nightmare.

"I went into lockdown. I had to think about what I am going to do here. I had a good friend, Richard, who came down and enlisted the help of a former policeman, someone who used to be on the Royal Protection Squad. They stayed several days because the place was surrounded by media and cameras. It was all terrible, emotional and all that. We were besieged for about four days.

"And then there was the funeral, of course, and cremation. Annabel, Annabel's sister, all the immediate family, Sophia and all that, probably about 20 people. The crematorium was in Salisbury about 30 miles away. We had a little service up on a hill near a small chapel. It was very sad. And of course on the way back it was like a Wild West scene. Like a bloody John Ford movie. There's a convoy of cars, like the nation's press were chasing us in our limos to get back to our place so we can get inside the compound and close the gates before they get there. It was a bit of a nightmare. But that's the way the media is.

"Nico died in August. Soon after the funeral, in September, I had a gig in Stuttgart, Germany, which I was obviously thinking of cancelling. But both boys said to me, 'Let's do this. We *need* to do this.' I wasn't worried about myself. I was concerned about my boys. It was the first thing we were able to do to solidify the family after the trauma of Nico's death. So we flew to Germany, and when we arrived at the venue it was cordoned off by a security fence made up of 90 Porsche Carreras: an interesting distraction all round.

"And again, that Christmas, I decided that we should go to South Africa, to Cape Town, just the three of us. I said, 'Look, I'm going to rent a house and I think we should go down there for Christmas. It's a great little scene.' We did and we got to meet great local musicians. We even did one little gig together. An unofficial little gig but we had a great time for two weeks and that was a kind of healing time, really. After that we were all pretty cool.

"It was obviously tough for everybody connected to the family. It was a tremendous shock. Unfortunately for me, or fortunately for me, it wasn't because I hadn't told anybody about the previous attempt. I didn't think it was necessary. Although I had mentioned it to Annabel, who poo-poo'd it. Funnily enough, there might have been something in what Annabel used to say about it. Because I can remember when Nico and I were courting as it were, sort of surreptitiously, and she took me to see this Swedish film, *Elvira Madigan*. It was about these hopeless lovers and in the end they blew each other's brains out. She was really into that movie, so it makes me think. But on the surface, at the party and all that, she was absolutely fine. We didn't have any worries, really. But obviously something was really wrong.

Photo 26: Georgie (far right) in Cape Town, South Africa with his two sons: drummer James (far left) and guitarist Tristan (second right) – between them is saxophonist Ezra Ngcukana.
Courtesy Clive Powell

"The awful thing when something like this happens is that everyone wants to pour out their grief on you. I got so many letters and that's what I found most of the time. But there were also some really interesting letters from very good friends of ours, close friends, Nico's in particular, and some she knew really well before she met me. One or two of them said, 'You know, she really did it right. She was really strong...' and all that. There was no stigma attached to it in some of her friends' eyes. Which kind of helped. I know it helped me.

"It was a terrible time. I thought that perhaps one of the best ways to deal with the grief, and also to help alleviate all the pressures and emotions, was to get involved with the boys and their music. So, after Nico died, the boys and I started to perform together, professionally, as a family."

In October, 1993, Georgie went into the studio along with his boys and some of the old Blue Flames and recorded an album, *Three Line Whip*. He decided to set up his own label, which he also called Three Line Whip, because the intention was to record the family music. There have been a dozen releases over the years.

After he recorded that album he was invited to New Zealand for a couple of concerts. He decided to take the boys, to get as far away from home as possible. They spent a couple of really happy weeks together there, distracted by the beautiful countryside, spending time with friends and playing three concerts. That's when the family trio really began to come together; they were experiencing intense moments together, both onstage and off.

There had always been music in the house, as there had been in Georgie's boyhood home. Both Tristan and James were drawn to music and spent hours away from their parents practising their instruments. The place was set up for casual jam sessions. Georgie had kitted out the barn with all the instruments and amplification you would need. Tristan was friends with Mary McCartney, one of Paul's daughters, and one weekend the whole family – Paul, Linda, Mary and their son James – came down to Hook Farm. It was an all-nighter in the barn, everybody playing and jamming. It must have reminded Georgie of the Flamingo all-nighters: that loose, happy, family thing.

Tristan started on piano but struggled with the mechanics of it – reading the notes, treble clef, bass clef – just as Georgie had. Georgie told him, "Look, don't give yourself any unnecessary stress. I had that problem as well. If you want to play, just play and have fun." The next week, Tristan came home with the violin. A few years later, it was a guitar and that's the chair he held in Three Line Whip for the duration.

James started on drums at age ten. Georgie had taken him to a Buddy Rich concert and, when Buddy launched into his 15-minute solo, James shot out of his seat, wide-eyed, grinning from ear to ear. Georgie had an old drum kit set up in the barn, and the next day James started practising. Georgie says, "Sometimes I still have to kick myself. I didn't want to embarrass him but I've openly said that he's the best fuckin' drummer I ever played with. He plays all the things I want a drummer to play exactly the way I want them to be played. Because he grew up with it and he knows it intuitively, he didn't have to learn it."

At first, Georgie tried to dissuade his boys from thinking about making a living out of music – for all the obvious reasons. But then, after playing together and travelling together, his mind changed.

"I was beginning to realize the potential of it," he says. "I was thinking that this would work, and it's fun of course, and it's within the family. And it's valid: nepotism didn't come into it because we don't take prisoners when we play together. There's none of that shit going on. It's all down to making it work musically and the ability to play. So, hey, what's wrong with this? Then I started to think I'm going to start looking for work with this group.

"The nice thing about playing with your sons is that it gives you a chance not to be the father. You can actually start a new relationship up on the stand," says Georgie. "Because, when you're there, it's all straight-ahead. There's an equality, apart from the thrill and the emotions and the adrenaline that you share. Whenever you're playing in a band you have that, but it's on a higher level still when you play with members of your own flesh and blood.

"Because of the solidity you develop on the bandstand, you feel you can actually surmount anything: nothing's too big; there is no mountain high enough," says Georgie.

A moment of proof occurred when they went to play a jazz festival in Jakarta along with trumpet player Guy Barker. They all flew from Hong Kong to Jakarta, but first another gig had been arranged in a town called Bandung, about a five-hour drive, through jungles, on a winding, dangerous road. After surviving the experience, they arrived in the middle of the night at the "hotel".

It was up a small side street. There was no entrance as such, just a little desk with a credit card sign, and nobody there to help. They took four keys and walked through the reception area into a small quadrangle where the rooms were. Barker took his key and walked up some obviously unsafe stairs, disappearing into the gloom. Georgie let himself into a small, dirty, damp stall. Then he heard a scream from above. "I thought, 'It's Guy', and I ran upstairs along this little balcony to where his room was and I went through the door of his room, and there's no roof. They had given him this room with no fuckin' roof on it. Just a broken bed in the corner.

"We went back to the gig and told the people we're not staying there. You've got to drive us back to Jakarta after the gig. But the drive back was one of the most nightmarish drives you can imagine. For like four-and-a-half hours it was just constant, nerve-racking driving through dark jungle on a highway with hairpin bends, with the driver overtaking anything in his path. I lost count of the number of times we nearly had a head-on crash. We arrived in Jakarta city for the morning rush hour so he finally had to slow down. It probably would have been better sleeping in a roofless hotel than making that trip."

In rugby, the player in the middle is called the hooker. The ball is passed into the scrum and the hooker has to hook it back to his side at which point play starts. In a sense, the hooker is the prime force. At the end of their gigs, when they take a bow together, Georgie stands in the middle of the two boys, like the hooker, and puts his hands around them as they take their bows. "To me," says Georgie, "it also symbolizes that the boys are actually supporting their father as well. They certainly got me through that harrowing trip and many others besides."

Around this same time, he started working with Bill Wyman. Bill had been getting restless after leaving the Rolling Stones and was thinking of putting a band together and doing something serious. But before that he was inclined to do something fun – not to take it on the road but to put a bunch of faces into the studio and go back to the music that started the stone rolling.

This is how Georgie became a founding member of Bill Wyman's Rhythm Kings. The band – which varies from five to ten pieces depending on the circumstance – eventually recorded enough material for three CDs: a real cross-section of blues-based material. Georgie sang a version of "Melody", the Billy Preston/Mick Jagger/Keith Richards composition, on which Eric Clapton played guitar. Bill also got Georgie to sing "I Got a Hole in My Soul", a one-off hipster thing that they used to play down at the Flamingo all-nighter. "I've got a hole in my soul ... everyone everyone everyone everyone, and my toe's sticking through..." In the Rhythm Kings, Georgie usually drew the more difficult bebopping things.

In April 1998, after all the material had been recorded, Bill gathered together some of the musicians who had been involved and formed the core of a road band, including Georgie on Hammond organ, Gary Brooker on piano and Peter Frampton on guitar. "Bill had a lovely backstory with Peter," says Georgie. "They were from the same part of South London. Of course, Bill was much older. When Peter was 15, Bill used to pick him up at his parents' house and take him up into the West End to have a listen to what was going on, and then take him back home safely, making sure he got home, all to give him a bit of experience.

"Bill had a lot of great musicians on the recording," says Georgie, "but we were the only ones crazy enough to go out on the road with him. Bill's got the lowest metabolism of anybody I've ever met: he's so easy-going, and it's common knowledge that, during all the madness with the Stones in the '60s and all that, he never dabbled in any drugs. He has a little drink of wine but he was never part of the drug scene and all.

"He's very level-headed and he's older than the rest of us. He did his National Service when none of the rest of us did. And he knows his own limitations as a player and, as we've said time and time again, bandleaders like to surround themselves with really good players.

"On a lot of the recordings we did in the studio, he'd be in the control room and we'd record without bass. He would make sure that he was absolutely happy with it, because a lot of it was being arranged and created in the studio at the time we recorded. Then, when he was comfortable, he'd go back in and record his bass. And, to his credit, when you listen to the CDs, you wouldn't know that. It all sounds like it was done at the same time.

"I admire his commitment to the band. I think he did it because he never got a chance to play that kind of music in his 30 years with the Rolling Stones. He missed it. And he knew there was a lot more to life than being in the Rolling Stones, so he quit and started a new life. I admire that," says Georgie. "We're playing the music of our childhoods."

About two years after Nico passed, Georgie met someone new. He was living alone at Hook Farm, which is quite a sizeable place. One day, he went into an antique shop down the road and was introduced to Suzi, "this creature with a charming face". The next day he rang her up and said, "Would you like to go out for dinner sometime?" There was a club in town not far from the railway station. He'd never been there but she'd seen in the local paper that Edwin Starr was playing and she had tickets. Georgie said, "You're joking! Great, let's go."

Years before, in 1967, Georgie had booked Edwin Starr at one of his parties in London. It was at the Cromwellian Club, one of his hang-outs, and Rik Gunnell decided to get some press out of the event by suggesting he make it a fancy-dress affair. He went dressed as Nureyev, Paul McCartney turned up as a Confederate officer and John Lennon came dressed as a priest; he had just made the remark about the Beatles supposedly being bigger than Jesus – taken out of context, but it was following him around the world – so his choice of costume was both ironic and timely. Everyone was in fancy dress and it was a fabulous party. Georgie had booked Edwin Starr just so he could hear him sing "Stop Her on Sight (S.O.S.)".

Photo 27: John Lennon (left) with Paul McCartney (right) shares a laugh with Georgie in fancy dress at the Cromwellian Club, 8 January 1967.

Trinity Mirror/Mirrorpix/Alamy

So, when his name turned up 40 years later, "I thought he might remember me from that evening," says Georgie. "In fact, he did. He spotted me and called me up. He had a great band, English guys, because he had moved to England, and he's whipped a showband together and it's like the James Brown Review. He's got a whole horn section, a big rhythm section and backing singers. He's up there doing the works and it's fantastic. That was our first date, she and I. We were both, like, 'Yeah, man. This is great.'

"I eventually persuaded Suzi to move in with me and there began, in my opinion, the most prolific and satisfying period in my life as a songwriter. We travelled together far and wide and I personally was happier by the day. I'd already bought a second home in Sweden and I had all the good-quality work that I could handle."

But, after nearly a decade together, as he wrote to a friend, "...my son Tristan had issues with his relationship and these began to have an effect on my own situation with Suzi ... (and) for a combination of reasons, including my own bungled attempts at resolving the situation, she decided to leave. I was devastated."

Years before, while in Australia with the Aussie Blue Flames, Georgie spent long hours talking into the night with trumpeter Keith Stirling about the inherent difficulty between men and women, describing how men have problems communicating with women and vice versa because of their different mindsets. "And I think probably as musicians it becomes slightly more complicated," he says. "I mean, men in any walk of life have connections with their occupations, some more intense than others. But music probably puts you in a more isolated position regarding domestic communication. You're in the centre of this circle, and they can't get inside that circle.

"It's one of the basic problems of understanding each other: she can't be in the band. Even if she's got great musical ears and understands every note that you play, she's not in the band. And the music does take up a lot of our time. It never really goes away. Even just the basic camaraderie in the band room, where outsiders don't know what you're talking about.

"It's probably the same with any close relationship with a member of the opposite sex. I've really only had three: Carmen, then Nico, and then Suzi. And there probably were difficulties with communication all along, but I wasn't even aware of it at the time. I was too busy keeping everything afloat, this mission in life, being the breadwinner and all the rest of it. Because there wasn't going to be any other career for me."

Years later, Suzi gave him the book *Men Are from Mars, Women Are from Venus,* which uses the metaphor of different planets to explain the fundamental differences in communication between men and women. Georgie subsequently wrote a song, "Mars and Venus", as his way of contributing to the conversation. "Not being able to do it at the kitchen table," he says, "I put it into song.

"Because, onstage, we confess. That's what we do. Every night on the stage, I'm telling the truth. I'm telling you the story of my life, every night, in public."

After the separation, he decided to spend as much time as he was allowed at his Swedish house, away from what he called "an unsatisfactory and rapidly declining UK". Both of his sons had families – they'd left home and were established – and Sweden had always been welcoming to him; he'd been working there for nearly 50 years.

"I make jokes about the fact that first I got out of Leigh and went to London – I got out of the coal mining, cotton, industrial belt and went to the big city. And then I moved out of the big city to the countryside. And now I've moved out of the country altogether. It's been a bit like the way it was back in the '60s, when fans were following the bands all over London and we were moving from club to club as fast as we could just to stay ahead of them.

"That's why, when I decided to buy a second home, I was comfortable that it was going to be in Scandinavia, in the opposite direction to where everybody else went. They all wanted to go down to France, Spain, Portugal, where it was cheaper and warmer. Now there are whole colonies of them down there. I went in the opposite direction, because I knew they wouldn't be there. They wouldn't dream of going there. And I wouldn't recommend it to anybody that didn't know the country, because it would be hard, just walking into a Scandinavian environment with a very strange language, not knowing anybody.

"It's fortunate to be able to do it all through music. There's no language barrier in music, and through music I've made lots of friends. For example, when I bought my house, I needed a lawyer. And the secretary of the Swedish Jazz Society is a sometime bass player. His job is an advocate; he's a lawyer. So I rang him up and he did the paperwork for me. And the fourth trumpet player in the local big band in my town, he's the carpenter. And the trombone player in another band that I work with, he's a professional painter. So the whole thing came together through music. The house has been fixed up by the jazz connection!"

While living there, his diary was as full as he wanted. There were many fine jazz musicians in Sweden and many strong jazz festivals. In particular, there is an annual festival in Stockholm, at Skeppsholmen, right on the water. It's very prestigious and Georgie had played it often. One year, he was invited to sing with the great Hank Jones on piano, Peck Morrison on bass, Alan Dawson on drums and Bill Watrous the trombone player, all giants of American jazz, right in his own back yard. He may have escaped England but he hadn't escaped American jazz musicians. "They were obviously from another generation," he said. "I was a young whippersnapper but to be able to be in their company and learn from these guys was incredible."

He and Lasse Samuelson also developed a project that they ultimately recorded as an album of songs suitable to be performed in churches, including "Georgia on My Mind", "Stardust" and a few other quasi-religious things. Lasse played "Come Sunday" by Duke Ellington, on the flugelhorn. All these beautiful melodies recorded with a small professional choir in Stockholm.

To promote the album, they booked a long tour in the middle of winter – six weeks in January and February – with snow everywhere, piled high, at beautiful churches in dozens of Swedish venues: big towns, small villages. A different choir performing with them every night.

"It was a wonderful experience," says Georgie. "I played piano. Lena Ericsson was my co-artist and, apart from singing, she also played the electronic keyboard, and Lasse played his flugelhorn. And those were the only musical instruments. The rest of the instruments were voices: our voices and the local choir voices. Some of these choirs sounded absolutely beautiful and almost reduced me to tears when I was singing with them."

In 2002, in recognition of his contributions to the Swedish jazz community, Georgie was honoured by the Swedish Executive Jazz Society. It came as a surprise to him, happening during a concert held at the Hotel Anglais in the centre of Stockholm. Halfway through the concert, the proceedings were brought to a halt and the President and Chairman of the Jazz Society came to the bandstand, delivered a speech about Georgie and presented him with an award which conferred on him honorary membership of the Society. There were only two other previous recipients of this award: President Bill Clinton – presumably for his efforts on the tenor saxophone – and the legendary boogie-woogie piano player Charlie Norman. Receiving the award cemented Georgie's relationship with his adopted home, Sweden.

He became a teacher at music colleges, in Sweden first and then throughout Europe. His first teaching experience had been in Holland back in the 1980s. At first, he didn't feel qualified. However, when he discovered they didn't want theory, they wanted practical experience – how he *actually* went about it; how *he* came to be where he was – he had a great time hanging out and singing with the students, sharing his stories about the jazz life. "Even though I'm not a qualified teacher," he says, "I'm certainly qualified to talk about this life.

"And it helps me put my own life in perspective. Because I've always done it without thinking. But when I'm relating it to the students, it becomes slightly more ordered. In Slovenia, to help the students get inside the process, I took seven or eight jazz CDs along, all the things that mattered to me in the whole scope of things – Mose Allison, Dizzy Gillespie's *School Days*, Ellington at Newport ("Diminuendo and Crescendo in Blue"), Jimmy Witherspoon's California concert with Ben Webster – and I said, "This is how I got started. This is rock 'n' roll to me. This is Dizzy Gillespie singing rock 'n' roll. And then it's just a matter of progressing from here." I played them Cannonball Adderley's "Work Song". I said, "This is dance music. It's as rocking as it will ever get."

And they all went "yeah", because they hadn't thought of it from that point of view. It's all connected.

"I found it was an interesting way to describe it to the students, and to myself, because I'd never actually had to describe it to anybody. So by doing it for the students, it started to make more sense all round. It relates to the fact that all the great jazz musicians began that way, playing blues or whatever you want to call it. A lot of young people aren't aware of this because they think that all these jazz geniuses started at their peak. But back in the '50s even Clifford Brown played in a band called Chris Powell and the Five Blue Flames, an R&B band, which is kind of scary how close it is to my own beginnings."

Gradually, he was seeing himself in the great chain of jazz, as a legitimate working participant in the jazz life, history made while you wait. And getting this distance – both physically and emotionally – from where it all went down also gave him some clarity and a sense of ownership in this deep American form. Through the challenges and personal risks he had taken, both on and off the bandstand, jazz had made him a world citizen.

"For me, it all comes down to the years when you first start listening to the music. You just played it and played it until you knew it. Everybody can hear it eventually, if you play it often enough, modern jazz, bebop, being, as Jon Hendricks said, 'The most eloquent way of speaking ever invented'. It's very articulate and intellectual, so it does take a while to cop it. But it's within most people's ability to understand it with a little bit of study. Of course, if you haven't got it, if you're not going to hear it, you know it. But if you *do* hear it, you're hooked.

"The Beatles and the Rolling Stones, they started with the blues, of course. But they didn't get into the intellectual stuff, or the hipper stuff – without sounding facetious, but that's exactly what it is. They just stayed basic and that's why the Rolling Stones are able to transcend the generation gap every year. The parents take the children and the children take their children, the grandchildren, the great-grandchildren, they all buy Rolling Stones tickets.

"There comes a time in everybody's development that you come to a crossroads. If you don't want to investigate it, then you can take the low road. Which is less interesting. But if you want to be adventurous, you can take the high road. Once you've taken the high road, you can always go back, but if you've only taken the low road, you might find it a bit daunting later on in life to try the harder path. But when you're young and in the position to do it, then why not have a look? There's a risk factor involved, but if you don't take a risk, you'd never know, would you?

"It's like the 'Lurps', the Long-Range Reconnaissance Patrol soldiers [LRRPs], that go deep inside enemy territory. They leave the base camp on their own or in small groups and the others might see them going, and they might even know *where* they're going, but they just didn't want anybody else around when they did it. They operate absolutely fine on their own. In fact, they are better off operating on their own. They could do the job safer and more competently.

"There is no excess baggage. No layers of REMFs (rear-end motherfuckers), the guys in the back office who have never seen any action but are throwing orders at them all the time anyway. They have a minimum of bullshit to weigh them down. And that's what attracts me about the Lurper: he's going into the jaws but he's not fazed by it. Maybe a hipster is just a Lurper in civvies. There's a thrill factor involved.

"Back when I moved to Somerset, we just happened to be on the flight path of the naval air station. And in the next village over the hill, where the local pub was, there were two naval officers, flyers in the Fleet Air Arm, Mike Sharp and Nigel Charles. Mike flew Buccaneers off an aircraft carrier and Nigel flew Phantoms. These guys were my age but they were very glamorous to me. Their flight path came over the garden on the way to landing, so I used to see them come and go.

"Of course, I had been into flying since I was a kid going plane-spotting. It's always had this attraction for me, something about the freedom of being up there, away from all the shit down here.

"Years later Harry Secombe, one of the original 'Goons', was recording one of his *Highway* television programmes in my local area at RNAS Yeovilton, and I was invited to be a guest. I offered to compose a piece of music dedicated to the Fleet Air Arm but suggested I needed first-hand experience of flying in order to get the piece right. Mike fixed two sorties with me, which I flew in a Hawker Hunter jet with all the gear on, g-suit, oxygen mask, everything. I had to have medicals and emergency training and all that. We did two hours in the morning and two hours in the afternoon. Exocet simulation at 350 knots, 50 feet above the water, approaching a warship. For a long while that experience was the pinnacle of my thrill-seeking.

"Then, years later, when I was on tour with Van Morrison in Florida, I went skydiving. We jumped out of an open Cessna at 15,000 feet. The plane climbed to altitude very slowly, in large circles. And even though I'd had this experience in the jet and I'm keen on all this kind of stuff, I started to feel very apprehensive. During the last few circles, getting up to 15,000 feet, I was having some doubts about whether I wanted to go through with it. I thought, 'I don't need to do this with my life. I think I'll just opt to go back down in the aeroplane.' But Suzi jumped first so I had to go. And the thrill was fantastic once you did it. You freefall for 10,000 feet, then you pull the 'chute and the rest is boring. When you land, the first thing you want to do is run straight back into the aeroplane and do it again. In 2001, I returned to Florida and took a course in flying single-engine aircraft, with a view to getting a pilot's licence.

"Finally, for my 70th birthday, I went wing walking. My son James, whose father-in-law has this aerobatic business, probably figured it was an apt little present for me, before I got too old. They use an old Stearman biplane, and there's a strut on the top wing, in the centre, in front of the pilot's seat and behind the engine. It's just a wooden strut, about five feet high, and they strap you to this thing. It's got a tiny seat, smaller than a bicycle seat, and you clamber up on the wing and then the instructor straps you in. You're harnessed in so you can move your head and your arms, and your feet and your legs if you want, but your body cannot move. But you still don't feel secure. And so off you go.

"It's a very short take-off. And then there I am, hanging on to this seat behind me, because there's nothing else to hang on to. You feel so insecure because you're strapped to this thing and you're at the very centre point of the plane; there's only the engine down there in front of you, and you're in front of everything else. Your face, because of the G-force, is being pulled back and you're flying over the treetops and the farms. Again, I could have backed down, but I felt this was a once-in-a-lifetime opportunity. It was like the culmination of my thrill-seeking. When you're up there, you feel the wind in your face and you're hanging on for dear life and you're totally exposed to the elements. It is quite an exhilarating feeling.

"When we landed, James's father-in-law told me, 'There are more people who have climbed Mount Everest than have gone wing walking', so I felt part of an elite club. I probably won't do it again. But it's a bit of a full circle, starting out as a boy climbing to the top of the Yoyo, seeing nothing but chimneys, to eventually being strapped to the wing of the plane, flying over the countryside, enjoying the vista."

Another shock to his system was the surprise birthday party his boys arranged for his 70th. "My sons are pretty smart," he says, "and it was the kind of thing they would enjoy doing, the subterfuge and the intrigue, but I was completely taken off guard. Everybody knew about it but me. I walked upstairs in the restaurant with James and there was a curtain up. And in a split second I was suspicious, because I'd been to that restaurant before and there was no need to have a curtain up if there's only five of us.

"James opened the curtain and I saw my sister and my sister's son and daughter, who'd come down from the north of Wales; Annabel was there, Cosima was there. My friend Richard, who'd helped me out with security when Nico died, was there. Also many musicians from the bands: Alan Price, Zoot Money, all these faces. It's all rushing in front of you at the same time, like a fast-frame thing, all these faces that are connected with you personally, which you don't expect to be there. So the heart starts pumping and the adrenaline starts flowing and, in a split second, I just turned on my heel and started to go back down the stairs. I just didn't want to be that excited, or that wound up. I was looking forward to a quiet family dinner.

"I went down three steps, stopped and composed myself and then walked back up. But the initial experience was pretty shocking.

"At one point I had to say something. I thought the Eubie Blake quote was probably the easiest way out. So I said, 'I'm overwhelmed and delighted to see

Photo 28: Georgie (right) in Mexico in 2012, with writer Clifford Irving (left) and Ben Sidran. Courtesy Go Jazz Records

you all and thanks to everybody for coming in. I'll get my revenge on my sons another day. And as Eubie Blake said at his centenary lunch, with a cigar in one hand and a glass of whisky in the other, 'If I knew I was going to live this long, I would have taken better care of myself.'

"But, lately, I *have* started to take it a bit easier," he said after the fact. "I don't work so much, and I don't see all my friends that I have, because I'm content to just be cool, you know? Originally, Sweden was just somewhere to go, a different environment to enjoy, relax, and all the rest of that. You've got a boat with an outboard motor. You can just take it across the fjords for the afternoon. But now I call Sweden my second home. No regrets. I'm happy when I'm there.

"The very few interviews that I've done, it always comes to that. They ask, 'Do you have any regrets?' And I say, 'Look, man. I've been more fortunate than most. I've had this wonderful musical education, playing with all the great musicians all over the world with no language barrier. I've had this cultural education because I've travelled the world. I've made all these lifelong friends through the music. From the north of Norway to the south of New Zealand, from Tokyo to California and all points in between, I've been there and played there ... And those are the rewards that you couldn't cash in."

In these remarks, along with the sense of resolution and accomplishment, there is also a sense of past tense, a nostalgia for a way of life that is passing in front of one's eyes. The gigs may continue but the road no longer leads to the original destination. Perhaps the bridge is out. Perhaps we are all hanging on for dear life, totally exposed to the elements.

Epilogue: Getting There

"As soon as I can find a way out of here I'll be gone."

In 2018 Georgie decided to move back to England. He had never become an official resident of Sweden – in fact, he would leave the country every three months or so, if only to maintain his status – and he was becoming concerned that he was a bit isolated living by the banks of the fjord. Relocating to England was a question of sooner or later, so why not sooner? Georgie had always exuded a sense of pride in being an Englishman, and a self-made one at that. Even during the wildness of the 1960s he had carried himself with a proper decorum, a respect for the British way of life; he was no revolutionary.

But soon after he moved home – to another farmstead two hours outside of London where he occupied the main lodging and kept the barn for guests and incidentals – he had misgivings. The country, according to his perceptions, was much further down the road to ruin than it had been before he left. The privatization of essential parts of the social contract, the railways, and the mishandling of crucial segments of the public services, key among them the medical system, had accelerated and he saw little hope for the future of Great Britain. Brexit had just been approved, a sure sign of the great dissolution of a greater international profile, and by the time the Covid pandemic hit, with Boris Johnson partying while everyone else remained sequestered, it was clear to him that "capitalism had failed utterly". Whereas politics in the past had been fertile ground for some of his hippest, most trenchant lyrics, it was now the wolf at the door.

The following excerpts are from our email correspondence:

> January 18, 2019
>
> Dear Ben ... I'm officially resident again in UK having sold my Swedish house as strategically, it was getting too big for me to handle (the garden mainly) but I've kept a nice little cottage just down the lane until this awful

political mess over UK/EU is sorted out – if ever! Our politicians have all (finally) shown their true colours (mostly yellow!) and are bereft of any credibility in my opinion and danger and uncertainty lie ahead globally. I suppose we, our generation had the best of it and on the gig front my diary remains full enough until year's end. The family trio continues to be in demand and I'm off to Hong Kong again in March. Big band concerts in May and a final run out with the Blue Flames at Ronnie's in September. Lots of other "fillers" in the gaps and I'm trying to resist doing a UK tour in Oct/Nov. Sydney OZ (the Basement) sounds more inviting despite the mileage. So it goes on! My "ticker" is still ticking and the chops remain in good shape although, due to balance problems, I sometimes need a walking cane. Enough of me. Sorry to have missed you last year and keep in touch. Love to Judy. Georgie.

PS. Those "Hipster" lyrics have new meaning.

We continued to make plans for another musical adventure. We didn't talk much about the balance issue. We both had heart issues and occasionally commiserated over that. But, as jazz musicians often do, we kept talking about the next new project, this time writing lyrics to Benny Golson's songs and recording them in New York with Benny and other members of his original Jazztet. Golson himself seemed amenable to the proposition. And Georgie, as always, was focused on contributing to the jazz canon; there was never a discussion about commercial success. It was always about the quest to make a bit of history, pay respects to our elders and swim in the deep and dangerous waters of bebop, "the most eloquent way of speaking ever invented". We planned to meet in London during my next stay at Ronnie Scott's to strategize. But then this:

October 28, 2019

In case you didn't hear, I had a bad fall and cannot reply to any comms until further notice (Xmas?!) GF

It turns out he had been in his home, up a ladder, hanging a picture when he lost his balance and fell. The picture hit the floor and the glass shattered; Georgie fell to the floor, fractured his right hip and severed several key tendons in his right hand on the scattered shards. The rehab of the right hand, allowing him to play piano again, began and went slowly. And Covid-19 was just around the corner.

April 19, 2020

Hello Ben. I hope the "lockdown" is working. Over here we're being led by overgrown schoolboys who haven't a clue! Same as most Western "democracies" I suppose and it's certainly going to be a long long haul. However, I intend to wade through your mail of last May on the book front during next week whilst everything is on hold. My bones are practically healed and I can drive myself around (where to?!) but my right hand is still a problem as far as playing to a professional standard is concerned although I practise a lot everyday. The hand surgeon was all set with Plan C, a minor op to get rid of the remaining scar tissue which is preventing the tendons on two fingers from working properly but Covid-19 means all bets (other ops) are off for the duration.

... On the Golson subject, I have to contact Benny over a possible copyright breach (unintentional on my part) concerning The Gypsy ... I wrote some lyrics to "Gypsy", not including the bridge part, as I realized the changes were almost identical to On a Misty Night. So I "threw it in" as part of Misty Night. Someone in Berlin recorded a gig with me and Alan Skidmore and released a cd!!! That version has been picked up and rearranged for recording/release by a Canadian vocalese group (something Bopsters). I'm trying to get to the bottom of all this before we all end up in jail! ... Yours in the Bunker and love to Judy. Georgie.

May 16, 2020

Hello Ben. Nothing much happening here as the days lose their identity and we have daily briefings/orders from a bunch of "head boys" masquerading as statesmen! Many Mose [Allison] pearls of wisdom spring to mind incessantly which in themselves are some consolation. I'm due a 120 mile round trip on Tuesday for a quick consultation with the orthopaedic surgeon who fixed my pelvis. This is pure "box ticking" and I'm loath to enter a hospital (they being amongst the most dangerous places to be in at the best of times) but the fact that I've been summoned might mean some kind of progress. The other surgeon who fixed (didn't!) my hand has written to say that he hasn't forgotten me and as soon as time permits (backlogs from hell) he'll try plan C (third time lucky!) to clear the scar tissue which is preventing me from playing properly. I sound like I did when I was 18 yrs old – minus the enthusiasm!

My spirits are not bad and I'm better off than most but like Mose said "I'm not downhearted – but I'm getting there"! As soon as I can find a way out of here I'll be gone. Stay cool. G.

PS ... was it Kurt Vonnegut or somebody similar that said "The light you can see at the end of the tunnel is that of an oncoming train!" Chin up.

August 18, 2020

... I just had op number 3 on my right hand and there is some improvement. I have to practise/play everyday in private to try to keep the scar tissue at bay which is more entertaining than boring physiotherapy exercises! I reckon I could now do a decent gig with the likes of VM [Van Morrison] or Bill W [Wyman] etc. but reserve judgement on being good enough to lead my own band yet. We'll see. Covid continues to affect all aspects of society and nobody is gigging anyway so I'm planning a little trip to the studio with two of my musical granddaughters. They like to sing ... with me amongst other things! Love to all. G

Due to Covid the next two years felt like they never happened. Gigs were shut down and the music business was one big ghost town. Finally, in 2022, I was back to playing at Ronnie's and hoped to see Georgie then. Due to scheduling conflicts, however, it never happened.

May 14, 2022

Hello Ben. I hope you're looking forward to resurrecting your European dates in June which I'm sure will be more than enjoyable. Alas, due to my post-Covid brain fog, I've made a major goof! I cleared my own diary and pulled several dates on health grounds until I sort out my balance problem. In fact the next gig that I'm hoping to do is a week at Ronnie's with Guy Barker's Big Band in September but the real bad news is I've booked myself a flight to Sweden to check on my house there and to make some important strategic decisions having not been able to visit for the last two and a half years. I booked the trip after checking the "snow storm" in my book where I'd stupidly not entered June 9/10. I'll be gone May 31st to June 15th and am mortified. If you can let me have the rest of the dates then I'll try and make it up (even with a chaperone!!) Yours in the doghouse. Georgie.

November 20, 2022

Hi Ben. Good to hear from you as always. Well, after a triumphant return to Ronnie's in September with Guy Barker's Big Band (12 shows sold out, Brother James on drums), I then "tested the waters" with the family trio at two old favourite venues. They also went well although my right hand is operating at 75% only in my opinion (I'm coming to believe that most of my surviving public/fans have cloth ears!) ... Fortunately I have a snooker tournament to watch on TV and will write again when things improve. Whatever next?!!) Love, Georgie.

Through it all, he continued to look to the future but despaired about England; he believed the warm community of his youth – a time of music and promise – had become compromised by greed and ineptitude: the trains, the medical service, the social violence, the racial prejudice. He fought hard to rehabilitate his hand and get back to playing piano. Playing gigs had always been his refuge from the world's madness. But the more serious underlying issue was his ongoing propensity to lose his balance. This had likely been a cause of his initial fall from the ladder; the unsteadiness had progressed, at first slowly, then all at once. Now he no longer felt safe onstage. By the summer of 2023, he was virtually housebound. Again, we planned to meet up in London during my time there but, at the last minute, it again proved impossible.

> May 31, 2023
>
> Hello Ben. Good to hear from you as always. Unfortunately I can't come to London as my mobility is seriously impaired and I'm in the process of moving home to a staircase-less dwelling across the "compound". I've had to cancel a week at the club with Guy's big band in July after suffering another fall in my kitchen! I'll be glad to fill you in on the telephone when you get to town. All the Best. Georgie.

We spoke. We continued to plan. We exchanged phone calls and kept spirits up. Two more years passed. And the physical decline continued. Again we talked about meeting at Ronnie's. It was as if the jazz club was some kind of promised land. Meanwhile, his doctor in London was gradually getting closer to making a diagnosis as to why his balance had become so bad and was rapidly getting worse.

Another year, another plan to meet up at Ronnie's, came and went. But then, a few weeks before the gig, he revealed that he had received the diagnosis.

> May 14, 2025
>
> Hi Ben, I'd dearly love to get up to Ronnie's on the Friday but not sure if my condition will allow. Hydrocephalus is the initial diagnosis ... I'm not completely wheelchair-bound yet but I'm getting there (copyright you know who). All options will be checked out.

Hydrocephalus is a progressive brain disease where fluid builds up, impeding one's physical coordination among other things, for which there is no cure.

> June 3, 2025
>
> Hi Ben. I'm having up and down days with my condition and was interested, even surprised to hear a public announcement by Billy Joel's people the other day on the BBC saying he pulled out of tour dates due to hydrocephalus. This is the first time as far as I know that the condition has been "declared" by a "face" so maybe the "chattering classes" and journos will all become "experts" on the subject in the near future ... unlike the medical profession! Yours Aye. Georgie

Then finally, in June 2025, after playing a gig at Ronnie's, Judy (my wife) and I went to visit Georgie, a two-hour train ride from Paddington Station in London. His son Tristan picked us up and drove us to the newish building into which Georgie had moved. It's a small, quiet and unpretentious place, and Georgie was still getting settled in. He looked remarkably fit for a man dealing with serious health issues – still the kid toughing it out on top of the Yoyo with a stray dog and a knapsack. Outside there was green rolling countryside and inside the cosy apartment his world of music, with many CDs and the radio, remained intact. But he was frustrated by his lack of physical mobility, bored by his daily routine. We talked about whether working on some music might be a good idea – there was a recording studio up the road where he could drop in to try out his chops – but it was such a heavy lift just getting out of the house that it seemed unlikely to happen. First things first: keep trying to sort out the health issues. Tristan brought in a nice lunch and, while the conversation was dominated by the tribulations of the local medical system and the constant drumbeat of bad news from the government, Georgie continued to laugh at life, whether to keep a stiff upper lip or to keep from crying one couldn't say. Somebody did quote the old blues lyric: "If I didn't have bad luck, I wouldn't have no luck at all."

After a couple of hours of trading war stories and paying respects to the past, Judy and I had to leave to catch the three o'clock back to London. As always, Georgie had been the perfect host, even though he was unable to walk us to the door to say goodbye.

The next day he wrote.

> June 27, 2025
>
> Hello Ben. … it was really good to see you and Judy and very much appreciated. As you witnessed, my mobility is very limited with no prospect of improvement alas, but I'll fight the good fight for as long as I can … Like Hoagy said "to get old is a big bore"! Keep in touch and we'll see if we can "close the book" before my brain shuts down! Yours Aye. Georgie.

The book you are now holding is the one of which he spoke.

I would like to thank the Hammond Organ Company for making my personal A-100 model (plus two Leslie speakers) and the people that transported it over the years to all the gigs, including the Routledge brothers, George, Brian, Martin, Alan and Billy; the South Western men, Robert Walker and Den Chilcott; Alan Berry; Steve Miller; Terry Sedgewick and Alf Dodd. And thanks to the dedication of my Hammond engineer, Clive Botterill, "the old girl" will undoubtedly outlive me.

Georgie Fame

About the Author

Ben Sidran is an American jazz musician, music producer, journalist and author, widely recognized as the host of National Public Radio's landmark jazz series *Jazz Alive!* and VH1 television's award winning *New Visions*. He has recorded 40 solo albums, including the Grammy-nominated *Concert for García Lorca*, and produced recordings for Van Morrison, Jon Hendricks, Diana Ross, Michael Franks, Rickie Lee Jones and Mose Allison. Sidran has written six books on and around the subject of jazz, delving into issues of race and music, the technological advancement of society, and how music shapes our lives. He holds a DPhil in American Studies from Sussex University, Brighton. See bensidran.com.

Index

References to photos are in ***bold italic***